LIFE-CHAINGING SERMONS

MATTHEW N.O. SADIKU

Copyright © 2024 Matthew N.O. Sadiku.

All rights reserved. No part of this book may be reproduced, stored, or transmitted by any means—whether auditory, graphic, mechanical, or electronic—without written permission of both publisher and author, except in the case of brief excerpts used in critical articles and reviews. Unauthorized reproduction of any part of this work is illegal and is punishable by law.

ISBN: 979-8-89419-209-3 (sc)
ISBN: 979-8-89419-210-9 (hc)
ISBN: 979-8-89419-211-6 (e)

Because of the dynamic nature of the Internet, any web addresses or links contained in this book may have changed since publication and may no longer be valid. The views expressed in this work are solely those of the author and do not necessarily reflect the views of the publisher, and the publisher hereby disclaims any responsibility for them.

Unless otherwise stated, scripture quotations are from the:

New International Version (NIV) of the Bible, used by permission of Zondervan Publishing House.

Scripture quotations marked KJV are from the King James Version of the Bible.

Scripture quotations marked NKJV are from the New King James Version.

Scripture quotations marked TLB are from The Living Bible.

Scripture quotations marked RSV are from the Revised Standard Version.

THE EWINGS PUBLISHING

One Galleria Blvd., Suite 1900, Metairie, LA 70001
(504) 702-6708

DEDICATED TO MY PASTORS:

Samuel Abegunde (late)

Olanrewaju Orundami

Ernest Essien

OTHER BOOKS BY THE AUTHOR

Secrets of Successful Marriages

How to Discover God's Will for Your Life

Wisdom: Your Key to Success

Choosing the Best: Living for What Really Matters

Enemies of Your Marriage

My Life and Work: An Autobiography

Radical Christian Living: By Kingdom Principles

Over One Hundred Loving the Word Bible Studies

Living a Life That Pleases God

God is With You: Enjoy His Presence

All Things Committed to Jesus

Traditional Medicines Around the World

Before You Divorce, Read This

Before You Marry, Read This

Imitating God: As His Dear Children

Matthew 1-15: A Pentecostal Commentary

Matthew 16-28: A Pentecostal Commentary

Mark: A Pentecostal Commentary

Luke 1-11: A Pentecostal Commentary

John 1-11: A Pentecostal Commentary

John 12-21: A Pentecostal Commentary

Romans: A Pentecostal Commentary

1 Corinthians: A Pentecostal Commentary

2 Corinthians: A Pentecostal Commentary

Ephesians: A Pentecostal Commentary

Galatians: A Pentecostal Commentary

Philippians and Titus: A Pentecostal Commentary

Colossians and Philemon: A Pentecostal Commentary

1 & 2 Thessalonians: A Pentecostal Commentary

1 & 2 Timothy: A Pentecostal Commentary

1 & 2 Peter: A Pentecostal Commentary

Hebrews: A Pentecostal Commentary

James and Jude: A Pentecostal Commentary

1-3 John: A Pentecostal Commentary

Revelation: A Pentecostal Commentary

TABLE OF CONTENTS

1. Radical Christian Living 3
2. Marriage Seminar 26
3. Selfishness in Marriages. 50
4. Unforgiveness in Marriage 66
5. Knowing God's Will 82
6. All things are Committed to Jesus – Part 1 111
7. All Things Are Committed to Jesus – Part 2 131
8. Keys to Effective Leadership 152
9. Time Management 187
10. Stress Management 211

Index. 238

PREFACE

This book consists of the power point lecture slides that I have used for church sermons or classroom teaching. People always ask me to share my power point slides after preaching or making presentation. I now make them available to everyone who may be interested. I hope it is useful to pastors, educators, or laymen who are interested in the topics covered. This book is organized into ten chapters with each chapter containing a sermon or presentation.

Chapter 1: Radical Christian Living: This sermon encourages Christians to live radically. Radical living is living differently from the culture. It is thinking differently, not like unbelievers. This is the way God and Jesus want us to live. We live radically by following the kingdom principles which consist faith, love, humility, righteousness, unity, influence, giving, etc. God is pleased with you and He blesses you when you live radically because you are doing what is right before Him.

Chapter 2: Marriage Seminar: This sermon reveals ten secrets of successful marriages. A marriage is successful when couple live together for the rest of their lives, with no divorce. A successful marriage has its secrets. First, couple must make Christ the focus of the marriage. Second, prayer is the divine rule for living and the family that prays together stays together. Third, we must be sensitive to spiritual activities and perceive when the enemy is at work. Fourth, there can be no unity and happiness in a home where there is no effective communication, which does not come naturally but be mastered. Fifth, every couple must understand their spouse's basic needs and be willing to meet them. Sixth, husband and wife should love each other deeply because love covers a multitude of sin. Seventh, commitment builds lasting memories and relationships with your spouse and children, the people you are most responsible for. Eighth, marriage may be regarded as a companionship in which each partner helps the other to grow to maturity. Nineth, we are good stewards when we prosper and profit from the use of money. Tenth, parents are to prepare their children for adulthood and eternal life. Unfortunately, most people go into marriage relatively uninformed about these secrets and struggle unnecessarily in their marital life.

Chapter 3: Selfishness in Marriages: This sermon regards selfishness as number one enemy of marriage and offers solutions. Selfishness affects happiness in marriage as it interferes with healthy selflessness which is the essence of marital love. It causes an inability to maintain a healthy loving relationship. It can lead to conflict, strife, infidelity, separation, and divorce. Selfishness is insisting on your rights, while love does not insist on its own way. If you pursue selflessness, you will enjoy your marriage and be happy.

Chapter 4: Unforgiveness in Marriages: In this sermon, we see unforgiveness and forgiveness as vital issues in Christian living and social interaction, especially in marriage. Unforgiveness is having a grudge against someone who has offended you. It hurts relationship and blocks flow of love. It may give room for the devil. Unforgiving people are their own worst enemy. Forgiveness is important for peace and unity. It is letting the offender off the hook.

Chapter 5: Knowing God's Will: This sermon addresses the important topic of knowing God's will. God's will is basically His overall plan for the individual/group and His step-by-step guidance in that overall plan. God wants us to know His will. He gave us the Bible to let us know His will. God has placed us in His body to do certain things and we need to know them. God guides using the Scripture, prayer, Holy Spirit, wisdom, mature council, providential circumstances, and supernatural means, which include dream, signs, visions, voice, angels, and spiritual gifts such as prophecy. Two or three combinations of these forms of guidance should be enough.

Chapter 6: All Things Are Committed to Jesus – Part 1: This sermon and the next one are based on John 3:35: "The Father loves the Son and has COMMITTED ALL THINGS into his hands." We consider seven of those things the Father has committed to His Son in this sermon and the remaining seven in the next. In this chapter, we consider: salvation, forgiveness, healing, access to God, mediation, advocacy, and judgment. God has committed all these things to His Son, Jesus. For this reason, Jesus Christ has many names and titles: Son of Man, Emmanuel, Messiah, Prince of Peace, Alpha and Omega, Light of the world, King of kings, Lord of Lords, the Creator of the universe, etc.

Chapter 7: All Things Are Committed to Jesus – Part 2: This is a continuation of the previous sermon. Additional seven things the Father has committed to His Son are: Names above all names, authority, good shepherd, light of the world, glory of God, King of kings, and Heir of all things. With this head-and-heart knowledge of Jesus, we should give Jesus the rightful place in our life. We should go into the world and share Jesus with others who are still living in rebellion.

Chapter 8: Keys to Effective Leadership: This presentation addresses the critical need of effective leadership at work, at home, at church, among colleagues or friends, in the society, etc. Leadership is now regarded as an art and something to be learned over time. An effective leader can lead people to the right destination. Followers naturally admire and respect the following ten qualities in an effective leader: (1) Living by the Kingdom Principles, (2) Fear of God, (3) Integrity, (4) Faithfulness, (5) Unselfishness, (6) Discipline, (7) Focus, (8) Servant heart, (9) Effective time management, and (10) Patience. Everyone has a measure of leadership potential but the measure varies from person to person. To rise to the challenge of being a leader is a lifelong commitment.

Chapter 9: Time Management: In this presentation, the importance of time management is addressed. Time management (TM) is making the most of your time and energy. It makes the difference between the wise and the foolish, between the rich and the poor. Time and energy management can make you more productive and reduce your stress level. Be tough with your time and prioritize. Actively avoid procrastination and time wasters.

Chapter 10: Stress Management: This presentation discusses stress management. Stress is the experience of being overwhelmed or unable to cope with pressure caused by outside events. Everyone feels stress at times; it is a normal part of everyone's life. Anything that puts pressure on a person and makes him feel overwhelming can cause stress; e.g. traffic, relocation, job loss, etc. Stress management offers a range of strategies to help you better deal with stress and difficulty (adversity) in your life. Managing stress can help you have better sleep and improve your mental health.

This is a must-read book for pastors or laymen who want to preach inspiring, life-changing messages. I trust that the book will become a valuable tool in their library. I acknowledge the support and cooperation from late Rev. Samuel Abegunde of Liberty Evangelical Church in Philadelphia, PA, Pastor Olarenwaju Orundami of Redeemed Christian Church of Church of God in Houston, TX, and Pastor Ernest Essien of Redeemed Christian Church of God in West Palm Beach, FL. This book is dedicated to them for providing me with the opportunity to exercise my talents.

- M. N. O. Sadiku

ABOUT THE AUTHOR

Matthew N. O. Sadiku received his B. Sc. degree in 1978 from Ahmadu Bello University, Zaria, Nigeria and his M.Sc. and Ph.D. degrees from Tennessee Technological University, Cookeville, TN in 1982 and 1984 respectively. From 1984 to 1988, he was an assistant professor at Florida Atlantic University, Boca Raton, FL, where he did graduate work in computer science. In total, he received seven college degrees. From 1988 to 2000, he was at Temple University, Philadelphia, PA, where he became a full professor. From 2000 to 2002, he was with Lucent/Avaya, Holmdel, NJ as a system engineer and with Boeing Satellite Systems, Los Angeles, CA as a senior scientist. He is presently a Regents professor emeritus of electrical and computer engineering at Prairie View A&M University, Prairie View, TX.

He is the author of over 1,230 professional papers and over 130 books including "Elements of Electromagnetics" (Oxford University Press, 7th ed., 2018), "Fundamentals of Electric Circuits" (McGraw-Hill, 7th ed., 2020, with C. Alexander), "Computational Electromagnetics with MATLAB" (CRC Press, 4th ed., 2019), "Principles of Modern Communication Systems" (Cambridge University Press, 2017, with S. O. Agbo), and "Emerging Internet-based Technologies" (CRC Press, 2019). In addition to the engineering books, he has written Christian books including "Secrets of Successful Marriages," "How to Discover God's Will for Your Life," and commentaries on all the books of the New Testament Bible. Some of his books have been translated into French, Korean, Chinese (and Chinese Long Form in Taiwan), Italian, Portuguese, Spanish, German, Dutch, Polish, and Russian.

He was the recipient of the 2000 McGraw-Hill/Jacob Millman Award for outstanding contributions in the field of electrical engineering. He was also the recipient of Regents Professor award for 2012-2013 by the Texas A&M University System. He is a registered professional engineer and a life fellow of the Institute of Electrical and Electronics Engineers (IEEE) "for contributions to computational electromagnetics and engineering education." He was the IEEE Region 2 Student Activities Committee Chairman. He was an associate editor for IEEE Transactions on Education. He is also a member of Association for Computing Machinery (ACM). His current research interests are in the areas of computational electromagnetic, computer science/networks, engineering education, and marriage counseling. His works can be found in his autobiography, "My Life and Work" (Trafford Publishing, 2017) or his website: www.matthew-sadiku.com. He currently resides with his wife Janet in Westlake Florida. He can be reached via email at sadiku@ieee.org

LIFE-CHAINGING SERMONS

MATTHEW N. O. SADIKU

Regents Professor Emeritus and IEEE Life Fellow
Prairie View A&M University
Prairie View, TX 77446
Email: sadiku@ieee.org
Web: www.matthew-sadiku.com

CHAPTER 1
RADICAL CHRISTIAN LIVING

(BY KINGDOM'S PRINCIPLES)

Presented by:

Matthew N. O. Sadiku
Website: www.matthew-sadiku.com
Email: sadiku@ieee.org

INTRODUCTION

Quiz:

Use one word to summarize the Bible.

WHAT IS RADICAL LIVING?

Answer to the Quiz – Kingdom, Love, Testament

There are two ways of living – culture or Kingdom principles.

Radical living is living differently from the culture.

It is thinking differently, not like unbelievers.

It is living with purpose, understanding why you are here.

EXAMPLES OF BEING RADICAL

Example 1: Giving your child a name Emeka, Femi, Mary, Esther – conventional

Glory, Mercy, Favor, Miracle – radical

Zechariah named his son John, a radical name (Luke 1:60-64).
John means God is gracious.

Example 2: Giving a new name to a church

First Baptist Church, St. Paul Church, – conventional

Community of Faith, Family Life, Covenant Fellowship – radical

Example 3: Hair treatment by women

With wigs, earn rings, and make up – conventional

Plain hair, without earn rings and make up - radical

WHY RADICAL LIVING?

(a) God demands radical living in the Old Testament (OT), God repeatedly asked His people to be different from other nations. That is why He gave His commandments and statutes. Consider examples of Abraham and Israel. God asked Abraham to leave his native home and asked him, "walk before Me and be blameless" (Genesis 17:1). God told Israel, "You shall be holy to Me, for I the LORD *am* holy, and have separated you from the peoples, that you should be Mine" (Leviticus 20:36)

(b) Jesus commands radical living in the New Testament. Jesus Himself was radical and He repeatedly commanded His disciples to be different from the Pharisees and Sadducees (Matthew 5:20; 20:25-28). He himself lived a different lifestyle. He said, "If anyone comes to Me and does not hate his father and mother, wife and children, brothers and sisters, yes, and his own life also, he cannot be My disciple" (Luke 14:26).

WHY RADICAL LIVING? - contd.

(c) **The way the disciples lived:** The disciples lived differently from those around them. At Antioch, they were called Christians (Acts 11:26). At Thessalonica, it was said of Paul and Silas, "These who have turned the world upside down have come here too" (Acts 17:6).

(d) **Your purpose for living:** If you are born again believer, your new life is expected to be different from the past life. You are a new creature and all things have become new.

If you live like others, you will die like others.

"If anyone *is* in Christ, *he is* a new creation; old things have passed away; behold, all things have become new" (2 Corinthians 5:17).

WHY RADICAL LIVING? - contd.

(e) For your own benefits: Living radically is for your own benefit. I will help you live according to God's way and experience heaven on earth.

"He shall live within God's circle of blessing, and his children shall inherit the earth" (Psalm 25:13, TLB).

HOW TO LIVE RADICALLY?

We live radically by following the kingdom principles.

Any kingdom must have four elements: (1) Land/territory, (2) A King/Ruler, (3) People/citizens, (4) Laws/rules.

- God has a kingdom. The kingdom of God is spiritual, relational, universal, and delegated. God is the King and we are His people living in the Kingdom.

- John the Baptist and Jesus and His disciples preached about the kingdom (Matthew 3:2, 4:17, 10:7)

Here, we consider seven principles of the kingdom we must live by.

KINGDOM PRINCIPLE #1 - FAITH

Principle # 1: Faith is the cardinal principle, the currency of the Kingdom. Without it, all other principles will not be effective. It requires faith to walk with God and dwells in His kingdom (Hebrews 11:6). The just shall live by faith (Romans 1:17). To walk closely with God, we must walk by faith, not by sight (2 Corinthians 5:7).

Examples of living by sight:

Example 1: Pregnancy before marriage

Example 2: Cohabitation – testing to see how things work out

Example 3: A marriage without children may lead to divorce

KINGDOM PRINCIPLE #1 - contd.

Examples of living by faith:

Example 1: Tithing by faith

Example 2: Daniel lived radically by faith

Example 3: The three Hebrew men in blazing furnace lived radically

KINGDOM PRINCIPLE #2 - RIGHTEOUSNESS

Principle # 2: Righteousness: Righteousness is doing the right thing. This is what the kingdom of God is all about.

"For the kingdom of God is not a matter of eating and drinking, but of righteousness, peace and joy in the Holy Spirit (Romans 14:17).

"Seek first his kingdom and his righteousness, and all these things will be given to you as well" (Matthew 6:33).

God demands that His people be holy just as He is holy and that means we should set ourselves apart for God's use.

But man's own righteousness is like filthy rags before God (Isaiah 64:6) and cannot please God.

When you accept Jesus as Lord and Savior and receive the Holy Spirit, the Spirit will empower you to live righteously and please God.

KINGDOM PRINCIPLE #3 - LOVE

Principle # 3: Love: Since God is love, love is the major key that opens His kingdom. Jesus summarized the Word of God by one word: love.

"'Love the Lord your God with all your heart and with all your soul and with all your mind.' This is the first and greatest commandment. And the second is like it: 'Love your neighbor as yourself.' All the Law and the Prophets hang on these two commandments." (Matthew 22:37-40).

As kingdom citizens, God expects us to love Him with your whole heart, soul, mind, and strength (Matthew 22:37-40).

KINGDOM PRINCIPLE #3 - contd.

We are expected to love one another as fellow believers:

"By this everyone will know that you are my disciples, if you love one another" (John 13:35).

We are also required to our enemies, love those who curse us and hate us (Matthew 5:44-46).

God has a reward for those who love Him:

"Eye has not seen, nor ear heard,
Nor have entered into the heart of man
The things which God has prepared for those who love Him"
(1 Corinthians 2:9).

KINGDOM PRINCIPLE #4 - HUMILITY

Principle # 4: Humility: We live in a society that demands human rights. As followers of Jesus Christ we must approach things differently. Humility manifests itself in our relationship: toward God, toward ourselves, and toward others (Micah 6:8). God esteems the humble (Isaiah 66:2) and opposes the proud (1 Peter 5:5,6). Paul said, "What are you so puffed up about? What do you have that God hasn't given you? And if all you have is from God, why act as though you are so great, and as though you have accomplished something on your own?" (1 Corinthians 4:7, TLB)

KINGDOM PRINCIPLE #4 - cond.

Jesus said, "Everyone who exalts himself will be humbled, and he who humbles himself will be exalted" (Luke 18:14).

Example 1: Humility is the litmus test that a man or woman is a servant of the Lord.

Example 2: God does not use proud people because He does not share His glory with anyone.

Moses is an example of God's humble servant (Numbers 12:3). John the Baptist is another good example (John 3:30).

KINGDOM PRINCIPLE #5 - UNITY

Principle # 5: Unity: It is sad to say the body of Christ is not united. Christians all over the world are so divided because of dogma, cultures, ideologies, and nationalities.

There is no biblical basis for a black, white, Hispanic, or Asian church. Jesus prayed that His disciples, including us, should be one in purpose (John 17:21-23). Paul said in Galatians 3:28,

"There is neither Jew nor Gentile, neither slave nor free, nor is there male and female, for you are all one in Christ Jesus."

God is calling us for oneness and for unity. He is reversing what He did for the towel of Babel. Unity in the kingdom produces unlimited power and enables a group of believers to do exploit. Building the tower of Babel is a classic example of what men can do when they are united (Genesis 11:1- 9). In view of this, Paul said, "Make every effort to keep the unity of the Spirit through the bond of peace" (Ephesians 4:3).

KINGDOM PRINCIPLE #5 - contd.

Jesus said, "If two of you agree on earth concerning anything that they ask, it will be done for them by My Father in heaven" (Matthew 18:19).

Example 1: Universal usage of English.

Example 2: The disciples were in one accord when the Holy Spirit descended on them (Acts 2:1, JKV).

Example 3: United husband and wife can do exploits (Deuteronomy 32:30).

KINGDOM PRINCIPLE #6 - INFLUENCE

Principle # 6: Influence: The word "Kingdom" means to have influence over a territory; and we are that territory.

As God influences us through His Word, we are required to influence the world in two ways: as light and as salt (Matthew 5:13-16). The Lord shows us how to influence the world for good.

Believers are to expose Satan and show unbelievers the way out of darkness.

Paul said, "Don't let anyone look down on you because you are young, but set an example for the believers in speech, in conduct, in love, in faith and in purity" (1 Timothy 4:12).

We influence others by exemplary living through our speech, conduct, love, faith, and purity.

KINGDOM PRINCIPLE #7 - GIVING

Principle # 7 – Giving: Giving is a basic principle of the kingdom. It is a service to meet the needs of others while finding meaning and fulfillment to our own lives. We should give tithes and offering to the Lord (Proverbs 3:9,10). We should never appear before the Lord empty handed (Deuteronomy 16:16). We should also give to the poor, widows, orphans, Levites, and foreigners (Deuteronomy 14:28,29).

When you help the poor, you are lending to God and He will repay you (Proverbs 19:17). Paul said,

"So two good things happen as a result of your gifts—those in need are helped, and they overflow with thanks to God" (2 Corinthians 9:12, TLB).

Our giving should be done without show or letting others know (Matthew 6:3-4). Our Father who sees in secret will reward us.

OTHER PRINCIPLES

These seven principles are not an exhaustive list. Other principles include:

- ☐ Prayer (Matthew 7:7,8; Isaiah 65:24)
- ☐ Worship (Matthew 6:1-16)
- ☐ Persistence (Luke 11:10)
- ☐ Focus or singleness of vision (Matthew 6:19-34, Joshua 24:15, 16)
- ☐ Wisdom (1 Corinthians 1:30, Proverbs 3:13-18)

BENEFITS OF RADICAL LIVING

Each principle has its own benefits.

(1) God is pleased with you and He blesses you because you are doing what is right before Him.
(2) God answers your prayer.
(3) You walk in the supernatural.
(4) Grow in godliness and become more like Christ.
(5) Become a better person, better husband, better wife, better children, better employee, better citizen.
(6) Less divorce among Christians
(7) Attract unbelievers to Christ

THANK YOU!

REFERENCES

M. N. O. Sadiku, *Radical Christian Living: By Kingdom's Principles*. Bronx, NY: Triumph Publishing, 2020.

CHAPTER 2
MARRIAGE SEMINAR

(SECRETS OF SUCCESSFUL MARRIAGES)

Presented by:

Matthew N. O. Sadiku
Website: www.matthew-sadiku.com
Email: sadiku@ieee.org

INTRODUCTION

There are secrets/rules in every aspect of life.

A successful marriage has its secrets.

A marriage is successful when couple live together for the rest of their lives.

A successful marriage produces a happy husband, wife, and children.

Unfortunately, most people go into marriage relatively uninformed about these secrets and struggle unnecessarily in their marital life.

"The secret things belong to the Lord our God; but the things that are revealed belong to our children for ever…" (Deuteronomy 29:29)

God reveals secrets to Daniel.

In this seminar, we will discuss ten secrets of successful marriages.

The first three are spiritual secrets, while the last seven are social secrets.

SECRET # 1 - CHRIST-CENTERED HOME

Marriage is a triangular affair: CHRIST-MAN-WOMAN.

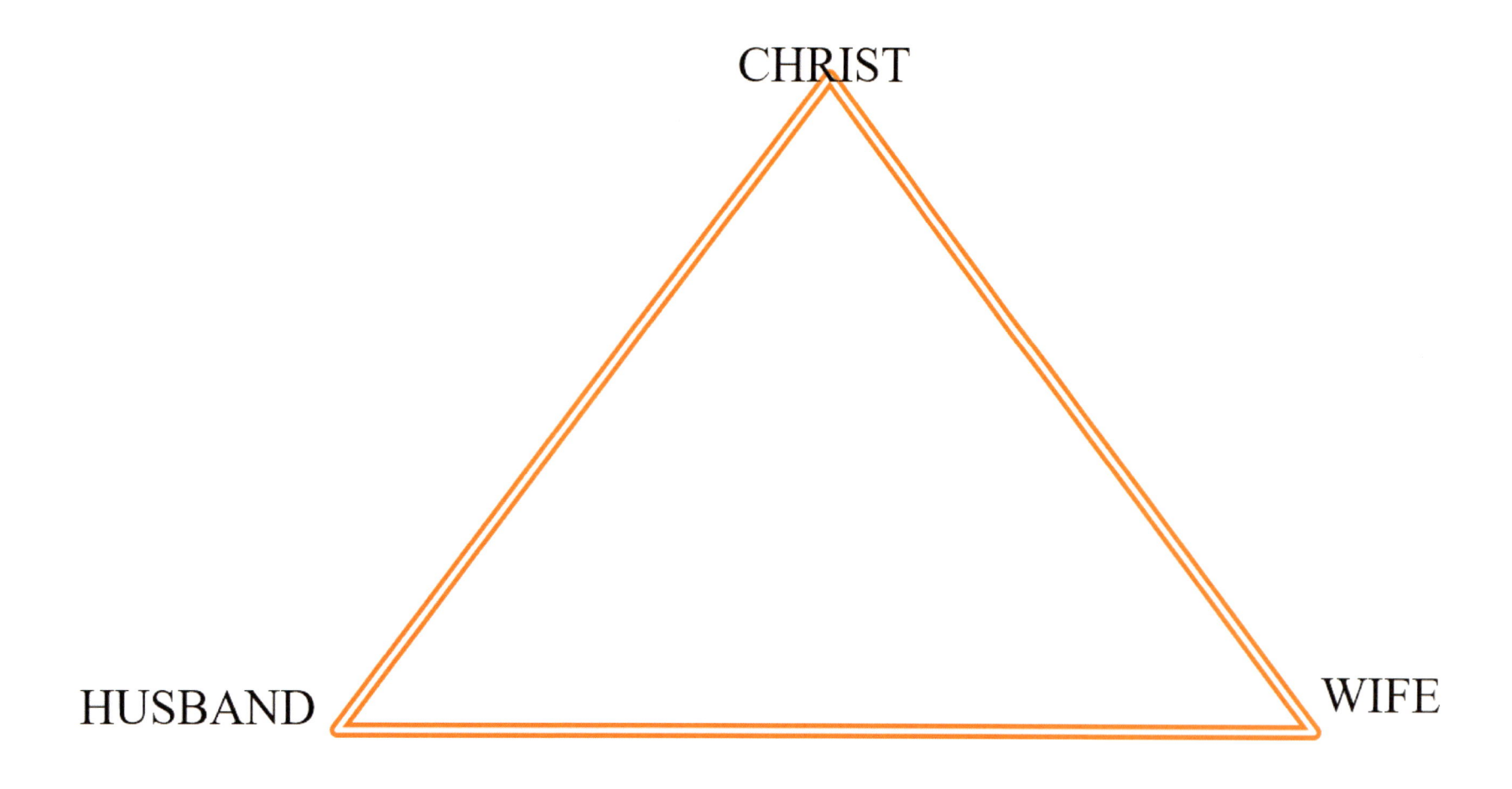

```
               CHRIST
                 /\
                /  \
               /    \
              /      \
             /        \
            /          \
           /            \
          /              \
         /_____\
   HUSBAND              WIFE
```

SECRET # 1 - contd.

ESTABLISHING DIVINE ORDER

- Jesus: He is the Master and Lord
- Husband is the head: to lead, provide, and protect
- Wife is equal partner: to submit, obey, and respect
- Children are to listen, obey, and honor their parents.

LIVING ACCORDING TO GOD'S WLLL/WORD

- by kingdom principles

MAKING CHRIST THE FOCUS

- what would Christ do in this situation?

SECRET # 1 - contd.

SURRENDER TO HIS LORDSHIP

"Why do you call be 'Lord, Lord' and you do not do what I tell you" (Luke 6:46)

FAMILY DEVOTION, PRAYING TOGETHER

"As for me and my family, we will serve the lord" (Joshua 24:15)

OBEDIENCE TO HIS WILL

"Not every who says to me, 'Lord, Lord' will enter the kingdom of god, but only he who does the will of my father who is in heaven (Matthew 7:21).

SECRET # 2 - PRAYER

Prayer is vital to a happy, successful marriage.

The family that prays together stays together.

Prayer is the divine rule for living.

A prayerless Christian is a weak believer because prayerlessness is the absence of the work of the Holy Spirit in a life.

Prayer is the key to the problems of our day, especially family problems.

James 4:2 says, "You do not have because you do not ask."

Jesus said, "Ask, and you will receive, that your joy may be full" (John 16:24).

SECRET # 3 - VIGILANCE

We are involved in a spiritual battle with the enemy - Satan (1 Peter 5:8).

Satan is the archenemy of God, of man, and of marriage.

Vigilance is paying attention to what is going on around us. We must be sensitive to spiritual activities and perceive when the enemy is at work.

We must be aware of the enemy's devices and not let him outsmart us (2 Corinthians 2:11).

"For our struggle is not against flesh and blood, but against the rulers, against the authorities, against the powers of this dark world and against the spiritual forces of evil in the heavenly realms" (Ephesians 6:12).

SECRET # 4 - COMMUNICATION

Communication is often the mission link in unhappy marriages.

It is the lifeblood of strong relationships.

There can be no unity and happiness in a home where there is no effective communication, which does not come naturally but be mastered.

Effective communication is the ability to say the right thing at the right time (Proverbs 15:23, TLB).

"Can two walk together except they be agreed?" (Amos 3:3).

The happiest couples are those who talk the most with each other.

SECRET # 4 - contd.

COMMUNICATION KILLERS:

- Anger (Ephesians 4:26,27)
- Selfishness
- Silence
- Wrong Words (Ephesians. 4:29)
- Wrong Timing

SECRET # 5 - UNDERSTANDING

Proverbs 4:7 says, "Wisdom is the principal thing; therefore get wisdom: and with all thy getting get understanding."

Understanding comes from reading the Bible and other books.

WHAT YOU NEED TO UNDERSTAND:

- Understand the differences in people:
    - Physical makeups, sex, emotion, family upbringing, etc.
    - You either value or not value the differences
- Understand your husband's needs
- Understand your wife's needs

SECRET # 5 - contd.

UNDERSTAND YOUR HUSBAND'S NEEDS:

- Significance
- Sexual Fulfillment
- An Attractive Wife
- Domestic Support

SECRET # 5 - contd.

UNDERSTAND YOUR WIFE'S NEEDS:

- Love and Affection
- Conversation
- Financial Security
- Honesty/Transparency
- Companionship
- Family Commitment

Every couple must understand their spouse's basic needs and be willing to meet them.

SECRET # 6 - LOVE AND APPRECIATION

We all strongly desire to love and be loved.

Sacrificial love (agape) is the hallmark of Christianity:

"By this all will know that you are My disciples, if you have love for one another" (John 13:35)

CHARACTERISTICS OF LOVE (1 Corinthians 13:4-8):

Patience	Kindness,
Lack of Jealousy/Envy	Endurance
Humility,	Respect/Courtesy
Unselfishness,	Good Temper
Right Morality,	Hopefulness

SECRET # 6 - contd.

APPRECIATING LOVE:

- Appreciation is a way of reciprocating love.
- Taking things for granted is the opposite of appreciation.
- Have a grateful attitude.
- Give compliments.

Love is a decision, not a feeling.

"Above all, love each other deeply, because love covers over a multitude of sins," (1 Peter 4:8).

SECRET # 7 - COMMITMENT

The Christian life is a life of commitment.

Ruth said, "Don't urge me to leave you or to turn back from you. Where you go I will go, and where you stay I will stay. Your people will be my people and your God my God. Where you die I will die, and there I will be buried. May the LORD deal with me, be it ever so severely, if even death separates you and me." (Ruth 1:16,17). This is a powerful statement of commitment.

Jesus said, "If anyone comes to me and does not hate father and mother, wife and children, brothers and sisters—yes, even their own life—such a person cannot be my disciple" (Luke 14:26)

Commitment is essential to the success of any group.

Commitment is what marriage vows are all about "for better, for worse… till death do us part."

SECRET # 7 - contd.

Jesus said, "A house divided against itself will fall" (Luke 11:17).

ENEMIES OF COMMITMENT

- Overcommitment to other things
- Adultery
- Selfishness
- Materialism & Worldliness
- Decadent environment
- Fear
- Lack of family goals and priorities

Commitment builds lasting memories and relationships with your spouse and children, the people you are most responsible for.

SECRET # 8 - MATURITY

Maturity is growing physically, emotionally, and mentally.

Maturity is unselfishness.

Marriage is a companionship in which each partner helps the other to grow to maturity.

God desires that we grow up and become mature (Ephesians 4:11-14).

A mature person possesses the following characteristics:

- Willingness to change
- Self-discipline
- Humility
- Patience
- Endurance

SECRET # 9 - FINANCIAL STEWARDSHIP

Money ranks high in problem areas in most marriages.

The husband and wife whose finances are a fiasco are a poor testimony to the wisdom and guidance of God.

The proper use of money is to prosper and profit by its use.

Fundamental position of the Scripture on money is that of stewardship.

A steward is one who manages another's property.

"It is [essentially] required of stewards that a man should be found faithful—proving himself worthy of trust" (I Corinthians 4:2, AB).

SECRET # 9 - contd.

PRINCIPLES OF FINANCIAL STEWARDSHIP:

- Giving God and government their parts first
- Laying aside for savings
- Staying out debt
- Budgeting and keeping records
- Investing wisely
- Setting goals, plans, and priorities in agreement

SECRET # 10 - PARENTING

Parenting is a difficult task God has given humanity.

Parents are to prepare kids for adulthood.

They are to prepare kids for eternal life.

Good parents are needed more than ever. They are usually loving, welcoming, and capable parents.

We can all improve by learning the basic ingredients essential to good parenting.

Parents are told, "Do not provoke your children to anger, but bring them up in the discipline and instruction of the Lord" (Ephesians 6:4).

SECRET # 10 - contd.

DUTIES OF PARENTS:

- Love the children
- Teach them
- Train them
- Provide for them
- Guide them
- Discipline them
- Pray for them
- Inspire them to greatness
- Help them to know God

CONCLUSION

We can summarize our discussion with 3 C's:

- Christ-centered home
- Communication
- Commitment

Yours can be a happy, successful marriage if you practice what you learn.

"Now that you know these things, you will be blessed if you do them" (John 13:17).

THANK YOU!

REFERENCES

M. N. O. Sadiku and J. O. Sadiku, *Secrets of Successful Marriages.* Bloomington, IN: iUniverse, 2nd edition, 2022.

CHAPTER 3
SELFISHNESS IN MARRIAGES

Presented by:

Matthew N. O. Sadiku
Website: www.matthew-sadiku.com
Email: sadiku@ieee.org

INTRODUCTION

Divorce rate is 50% in America.

Problem areas include:

Selfishness, Lack of love & Affection, Materialism, Worldliness, Overcomitment, Irresponsibility, Infidelity, Nagging & Criticism, Unforgiveness, the Devil, etc.

Selfishness is No. 1 enemy of marriage.

WHAT IS SELFISHNESS?

Selfishness is insisting on your way or insisting on your rights.

In our society, selfishness reigns.

A selfish person always wants things done his/her way.

Love does not insist on its own way (1 Corinthians 13:5).

Paul said, "Don't be selfish; don't live to make a good impression on others. Be humble, thinking of others as better than yourself" (Philippians 2:3,4, TLB).

MANIFESTATION OF SELFISHNESS

He cares only about his needs in bed.

He is only interested in what pleases him; he does not help with the house chores.

He interrupts you when speak.

He cares more about career than character.

Even when he realizes he is wrong, he does not know how to apologize and ask for forgiveness.

She always blames others for her failures and thinks she is ok.

She is sentimental, not objective.

She hides something she is ashamed of.

MANIFESTATION - contd.

Making decision without carrying others along

Not praying together

Having separate bank accounts

Pursuing separate goals

Not agreeing on the number of children to have

One eats meat while another eats chicken

One lives in Africa while the other lives in America

Living as if the other partner doesn't exist

Like a babe, thinking as if the world revolves around them

MANIFESTATION - contd.

Covetousness – preferring what others have

Greediness – grabbing more than necessary

Manipulation – being calculative and controlling, influencing others for one's own purposes, e.g. Jacob

Manipulation for men is money, for women is sex

Dishonesty – telling lies and deceiving others

Always has a hidden agenda – selfish ambition

MANIFESTATION - contd.

Hidden agenda – A man who brought his wife from Nigeria and trained her as a nurse so that he can be collecting her salaries.

Unrealistic and unreasonable expectations

Bribery & Corruption

Selfishness is a huge problem in Nigeria leaders

(3 Nigerians stealing 3 trillion Naira - greediness)

Those who live in the flesh are controlled by the carnal mind (flesh), which is self-centered. See Galatian 5:19-21

EFFECTS OF SELFISHNESS

It threatens oneness/unity in marriage. Cannot achieve much.

It prevents a couple from having the same goals.

It repels others from you and creates an atmosphere of hatred.

It makes it difficult to compromise.

It leads to marital problems such as sexual issues, communication, and in-law issues.

Example: A Nigerian women stealing part of food money to build a house without her husband knowing about it.

It leads to arrogance, which God hates.

EFFECTS - contd.

It affects happiness in marriage as it interferes with healthy selflessness which is the essence of marital love.

It causes an inability to maintain a healthy loving relationship. Divorce after divorce.

It can prevent parents from being responsible for their kids.

It can lead to conflict, strife, infidelity, separation, and divorce.

One is easy target for get-rich-quick schemes.

It can lead to frustration when one cannot have his way.

It may lead to adultery, running away, break marriage vows, and eventually lead to divorce.

It hinders prayer since God hates selfishness.

EFFECTS - contd.

It may be a cause of unforgiveness.

Selfish people live on the fast line and may die prematurely or commit suicide.

Not living by faith e.g. pregnant before marriage

Leads to cohabitation – living together with no commitment.

Claiming, "God told me." Using God's name in vain.

Short-sightedness – what I can gain now.

Selfish people are not good material for marriage.

They don't listen to correction.

SOLUTION TO SELFSHNESS

1. **Pray for Forgiveness:** Selfishness is a sin against God and your spouse. God judges selfish people. Ask for the forgiveness of your spouse and God.

2. **Love:** Selfishness is insisting on your rights, while love does not insist on its own way (1 Corinthians 13:5). Selfishness is all about getting, while love is all about giving.

3. **Prioritize Your Spouse:** Learn to put yourself second and prioritize your partner's needs before your own. Paul said, "For none of us lives for ourselves alone, and none of us dies for ourselves alone" (Romans 14:7).

SOLUTION - contd.

4. **Fight Against Pride:** Remember that everything you have including your spouse comes from God. Paul said,

   "For who makes you different from anyone else? What do you have that you did not receive? And if you did receive it, why do you boast as though you did not?" (1Corinthians 4:7).

   Humble yourself – God opposes the proud, but exalts the humble

5. **Learn to Compromise:** Learn to give and take.

6. **Be selfless:** Crucify self (Galatians 2:20). Do not think you are better than others (Romans 12:3). Think of what to give your spouse, not what to get.

7. **Be United:** Learn to do things together. Work like a team. Be of one mind.

SOLUTION - contd.

8. **Pray together:** The family that prays together stays together. Put God first and your family second.

9. **Be a blessing** – Giving instead of getting, be a river, not a pool. Sow and reap.

10. **Look up to Jesus** – Jesus is our example (1 Peter 2:21) and our role model. In whatever you do, ask yourself: "What will Jesus do?"

CONCLUSION

Selfishness is insisting on your way.

Perhaps there is no better place where selfishness manifests itself more than in a marital relationship.

Selfishness is the number one enemy of marriage.

Being selfish is one of the worst character traits one may possess.

Act more like a teammate and less like an adversary in your marriage.

If you pursue selflessness, you will enjoy your marriage and be happy.

THANK YOU!

REFERENCES

M. N. O. Sadiku, *Enemies of Your Marriage*. Bloomington, IN: Trafford Publishing, 2018, Chapter 1.

M. N. O Sadiku and J. O. Sadiku, *Selfishness: Its Impact on Marriage and Relationships*. Authors KD Publishing, 2024.

CHAPTER 4
UNFORGIVENESS IN MARRIAGE

Presented by:

Matthew N. O. Sadiku
Web: www.matthew-sadiku.com
Email: sadiku@ieee.org

INTRODUCTION

Unforgiveness and forgiveness are vital issues in Christian living and social interaction, especially in marriage.

Peter came to Jesus and asked, "Lord, how many times shall I forgive my brother or sister who sins against me? Up to seven times?" Jesus answered, "I tell you, not seven times, but seventy-seven times" (Matthew 18:21,21).

"If you forgive those who sin against you, your heavenly Father will forgive you. But if you refuse to forgive others, your Father will not forgive your sins" (Matthew 6:14-15).

WHAT IS UNFORGIVENSS?

Unforgiveness is having a grudge against someone who has offended you.

In an imperfect world, you will offend or be offended by someone: your spouse, relatives, friends, co-workers, brethren, etc.

When somebody offends you, consider John Wiley's saying:

"In essentials, unity; in non-essentials, liberty; in all things, charity."

- Essentials (praying together, saving, tithing)
- Non-essentails (offering, food)
- "Can two walk together except the agree?" (Amos 3:3)

I WHAT IS UNFORGIVENSS? - contd.

"He who cannot forgive others break the bridge over which he must pass himself" - G. Hurbert

"Be tolerant of one another and forgive each other if anyone has a complaint against another. Just as the Lord has forgiven you, you also should forgive"(Colossians 3:13).

"If you would increase your happiness and prolong your life, forget your neighbor's faults…. Forget the peculiarities of your friends, and only remember the good points which make you fond of them…. Obliterate everything disagreeable from yesterday; write upon today's clean sheet those things lovely and lovable." - Anonymous

WHAT IS UNFORGIVENSS? - contd.

Example 1: A woman who still remembered what her husband did 36 years ago. She divorced and suffered depression and loneliness.

Example 2: A man who would not allow his wife to join politics in Nigeria. He died shortly after their separation.

Example 3: An elder in the church who refused to forgive his wife. He went to Nigeria, became sick, and died there.

RECONCILIATION & FORGIVENESS

In Matthew 18:15-17, Jesus gives a procedure on how we are to reconcile and seek peace when we are offended.

"If your brother or sister sins, go and point out their fault, just between the two of you. If they listen to you, you have won them over. But if they will not listen, take one or two others along, so that 'every matter may be established by the testimony of two or three witnesses.' If they still refuse to listen, tell it to the church; and if they refuse to listen even to the church, treat them as you would a pagan or a tax collector."

ROOT CAUSES OF UNFORGIVENESS

(1) Offense

(2) Disappointment

(3) Giving room for grudges

(4) Hatred

(5) Pride

(6) Selfishness

(7) Lack of fear of God

WHY YOU MUST FORGIVE

(a) Forgiveness is important for peace and unity.

(b) God gave us people (relatives, spouse, friends, etc.) as special gifts. We must treat them as such.

(Imagine President Obama gives you his daughter in marriage. How would you treat her?)

(c) Forgiveness is a God-like trait

(d) Unforgiveness gives room for the devil

(e) Unforgiveness is a sin. It is hatred

(f) Unforgiving people are their own worst enemy

(g) Do not marry if you cannot forgive

CONSEQUENCIES OF UNFORGIVENESS

The consequences of unfrogiveness are deadly and detrimental.

(a) Festers into bitterness and resentment

(b) Hurts relationship and blocks flow of love

(c) Causes spiritual and physical damage

(d) Steals your joy of salvation

(e) Hinders prayer (Matthew 5:24; 18:35)

"If you forgive those who sin against you, your heavenly Father will forgive you. But if you refuse to forgive others, your Father will not forgive your sins" (Matthew 6:14-15).

CONSEQUENCIES - contd.

(f) May lead to revenge —e.g. A man inflates the tires of his wife's car.

   Vengeance belongs to God (Romans 12:19)

(g) Beating your wife/Not respecting your husband

(h) May lead to separation and divorce

GOD WANTS YOU TO FORGIVE

Forgiveness is vital to our relationship with God.

(a) God demands forgiveness. In the Lord's prayer:

"And forgive us our debts, as we forgive our debtors" (Matthew 6:12)

(b) Jesus demands forgiveness.

-In Matthew 18:21-35, Jesus gives a lengthy parable to illustrate the need for believers to forgive one another. A forgiven servant refuses to forgive another servant. Jesus concludes by saying:

"That's what my heavenly Father will do to you if you refuse to forgive your brothers and sisters from your heart" (Matthew 18:35).

GOD WANTS FORGIVENESS - contd.

(c) Not to forgive shows that we do not know God & How He operates.

(d) If you follow God wholeheartedly, with undivided heart, you will easily forgive others, especially your spouse.

(e) You should seek forgiveness from God and others.

(f) Repent. Unforgiveness is a sin.

> Paul said, "Be kind to each other, tenderhearted, forgiving one another, just as God has forgiven you because you belong to Christ" (Ephesians 4:32, TLB).

(g) Unconditional/advance forgiveness is the ideal.

Make forgiveness an ally of your marriage so that your marriage can last and be happy.

FORGIVENESS

Forgiving is the way to deal with unforgiveness. Some of the characteristics of forgiveness include the following:

- Forgiveness is letting the offender off the hook.
- Forgiveness is returning to God the right to take care of justice.
- Forgiveness is letting the offense recur again and again.
- Forgiveness involves not raising the matter again.
- Forgiveness involves change.
- Forgiveness is an indication of true healing.
- Forgiveness takes time. Give yourself time to heal.

CONCLUSION

(a) We have been called to higher standard

(b) The glory of God is at stake

(c) Be quick to forgive and learn to say "sorry"

(d) Love covers a multitude of sins (1 Peter 4:8)

(e) Never seek revenge

(f) Love your enemy

(g) Pray for your enemy

QUESTION?

REFERENCES

M. N. O. Sadiku and J. O. Sadiku, *Enemies of Your Marriage*. Las Vegas, NV: Book Films Media, 2nd edition, 2024, Chapter 10.

CHAPTER 5
KNOWING GOD'S WILL

Presented by:

Matthew N. O. Sadiku
Website: www.matthew-sadiku.com
Email: sadiku@ieee.org

MEANING OF GOD'S WILL

God's will has two-fold meaning:

(1) Overall plan of God for the individual/group.

(2) Step-by-step guidance in that blueprint or overall plan

WHEN WE NEED TO KNOW GOD'S WILL

(1) Choosing who to marry

(2) Right career

(3) Job offers

(4) Relocation

(5) Service (e.g. serving on a board)

People seek guidance in wrong ways: palm reading, fortune telling, voo-doo, astrology, horoscope, Ifa oracle, etc. – All of which are not God's way.

IMPORTANCE OF KNOWING GOD'S WILL

(1) God wants us to know His will. He gave us the Bible to let us know His will (Deuteronomy 29:29).

(2) God also gave us the Holy Spirit to guide us.

"For those who are led by the Spirit of God are the children of God" (Romans 8:14).

(3) God has a purpose for every redeemed person.

God has placed us in His body to do certain things and we need to know them (Roman 12:6; Eph.4:7,12).

(4) To please God so that He may be pleased with us.

IMPORTANCE - contd.

(5) Knowing God's will removes jealousy in your life. John said, "He must become greater; I must become less" (John 3:30).

(6) Only those who do His will on earth will enter God's kingdom.

"Not everyone who says to me, 'Lord, Lord,' will enter the kingdom of heaven, but only the one who does the will of my Father who is in heaven" (Matthew 7:21). See also Matthew 12:50.

People perish for not knowing God's will (Proverbs 29:18).

(8) God's will is a necessity, like food. Jesus said, "My food is to do the will of him who sent me and to finish his work" (John 4:34, 5:30; 6:38).

(9) God's will is needed for success – David always sought God's approval before embarking on any war and he always won.

IMPORTANCE - contd.

(10) Not doing God's will leads to failure.

At Babel, men could not achieve their goal because it was not God's will (Genesis 11:1-7).

Jonah headed to Tarshish when God sent him to Nineveh and failed (Jonah 1 & 2).

The key to failure is working against God's will.

Abijah told Jeroboam, "God is with us; he is our leader…. People of Israel, do not fight against the LORD, the God of your ancestors, for you will not succeed" (2 Chronicles 13:12).

The key to success is seeking God's will in all endeavors. David did this and won all his battles (2 Samuel 5:19,23).

PERSPECTIVES ON GOD'S WILL

From Revelation viewpoint: God's will is either secret or revealed. "Surely the Sovereign LORD does nothing without revealing his plan to his servants the prophets" (Amos 3:7). See also Deut. 29:29. The Bible is God's revealed will. When Jesus is coming or when you will die is God's secret will.

From Divine intervention viewpoint: God's will is either desired or determined. God's desired will requires human cooperation, but His determined will does not. God revealed His determined will to Joseph (Genesis 41:25,32). (See also Isaiah 14:26,27; 46:9-11). It is God's desired will that a man should be monogamous.

PERSPECTIVES - contd.

From Scope viewpoint: God's will is either general or specific. God's general will is love, wisdom, justice, holiness, kindness, good works, etc. It is God's general that we humble ourselves and live a holy life (Micah 6:8). His specific will for Joseph was revealed to him in a dream (Genesis 37:5).

From Degree viewpoint: God's will is either perfect or permissive. God permitted Israel to choose a king (1 Samuel 8:7). It was His perfect will that David became king (Acts 13:22). The birth of Ishmael was God's permissive will, while that of Isaac was God's perfect will.

CHARACTERISTICS OF GOD'S WILL

(1) God's revealed will is progressive, one step at a time. "A person's steps are directed by the LORD" (Proverbs 20:24). See also Isaiah 48:17, NLT.

(2) God's will is dynamic. For example, God directed David differently in 2 Samuel 5:19,30.

"The LORD, the God of Israel, declares: 'I promised that members of your family would minister before me forever.' But now the LORD declares: 'Far be it from me! Those who honor me I will honor, but those who despise me will be disdained" (1 Samuel. 2:30).

God changed His ways of dealing with man from Old Testament (OT) to New Testament (NT).

CHARACTERISTICS - contd.

Church leaders have not being dynamic but rigid on many issues, e.g.

(1) Women leadership in the church is proper now, not rigidly following what Paul said (1Corinthians 14:34). But Paul also said, "There is neither Jew nor Gentile, neither slave nor free, nor is there male and female, for you are all one in Christ Jesus" (Galatians. 3:28). See also Colossians 3:11.

(2) Use of King Jame Version (KJV) of the Bible, ignoring over 50 modern translations.

(3) God's will is desirable/noble.

"If any one aspires to the office of bishop, he desires a noble task" (1 Timothy, 3:1, RSV).

CHARACTERISTICS - contd.

(4) **God's will is good.**

"For I know the plans I have for you, says the Lord. They are plans for good and not for evil, to give you a future and a hope" (Jeremiah 29:11). See also Philippians 2:13.

(5) **God's will is timely** (at appointed time).

"When the right time came, God sent his Son" (Galatians 4:4). See also Daniel 11:27,29,35.

(6) **God's will can be missed** through stubbornness and disobedience (Psalm 32:8,9).

"Demas has deserted me because he loves the things of this life and has gone to Thessalonica" (2 Timothy 4:10).

"Stay always within the boundaries where God's love can reach and bless you" (Jude 21, TLB).

PREREQUISITES FOR KNOWING GOD'S WILL

(1) Salvation – God reveals His will only to His children.

(2) Surrender – We must not be stubborn like Jonah.

"Do not be like a senseless horse or mule that needs a bit and bridle to keep it under control" (Psalm 32:9).

(3) Separation – We must be separated from sin.

"God's will is for you to be holy, so stay away from all sexual sin" (1 Thessalonians 4:3).

PREQUISITES - contd.

Jesus prayed, "They do not belong to this world any more than I do. Make them holy by your truth; teach them your word, which is truth" (John 17:16,17).

(4) Seeking to Know it - Make effort to seek God's will through prayer and fasting. "If you look for me wholeheartedly, you will find me" (Jeremiah 29:13, NLT). See also Proverbs 8:17.

(5) Spiritual mindedness. - We must be spiritually sensitive or God-conscious.

"God is spirit, and his worshipers must worship in the Spirit and in truth" (John 4:24).

"The person without the Spirit does not accept the things that come from the Spirit of God but considers them foolishness, and cannot understand them because they are discerned only through the Spirit" (1 Corinthians 2:14).

HOW GOD GUIDES

(1) From Scripture – primary source. Read and meditate on it. God's will must align with His Word.

"Your word is a lamp for my feet, a light on my path" (Psalm 119:105).

"Keep this Book of the Law always on your lips; meditate on it day and night, so that you may be careful to do everything written in it. Then you will be prosperous and successful" (Joshua 1:8).

When you know the law, instructions, and promises and eternal plan for our lives, it becomes easy to do God's will.

HOW GOD GUIDES - contd.

(2) Prayer – This is the most conductive environment for hearing from God.

"If you want to know what God wants you to do, ask him, and he will gladly tell you, for he is always ready to give a bountiful supply of wisdom to all who ask him; he will not resent it" (James 1:5, TLB). See also Matthew 7:7.

Abraham's servant prayed for God's guidance in seeking for a wife for his master and God answered him (Genesis 24:12-14;42-44). He said,

"LORD, God of my master Abraham, if you will, please grant success to the journey on which I have come" (Genesis 24:42).

HOW GOD GUIDES - contd.

(3) Holy Spirit – If you are born again, you have the Holy to guide you. This is the main difference Christianity and other religions.

"When he, the Spirit of truth, comes, he will guide you into all the truth. He will not speak on his own; he will speak only what he hears, and he will tell you what is yet to come" (John 16:13).

"For those who are led by the Spirit of God are the children of God" (Romans 8:14).

HOW GOD GUIDES - contd.

(4) Wisdom – This is manifested in common sense and integrity.

"The integrity of the upright guides them" (Proverbs 11:3).

"Now the overseer is to be above reproach, faithful to his wife, temperate, self-controlled, respectable, hospitable, able to teach" (1 Timothy 3:2).

"He who loves wisdom loves his own best interest and will be a success" (Proverbs 19:8, TLB).

HOW GOD GUIDES - contd.

(5) Mature Counsel - Advice (other people's experience) from seniors, loved ones, or even servants,

"Get all the advice you can and be wise the rest of your life" (Proverbs 19:20, TLB).

"Don't go ahead with your plans without the advice of others; don't go to war until they agree" (Proverbs 20:18, TLB).

"Plans go wrong with too few counselors; many counselors bring success" (Proverbs 15:22).

Naaman's servant advised him (2 Kings 5:3).

HOW GOD GUIDES - contd.

(6) **Providential Circumstances** – God orchestrates events and guides using open/closed doors.

"We know that in all things God works for the good of those who love him, who have been called according to his purpose," (Romans 8:28).

"He makes me lie down in green pastures, he leads me beside quiet waters, he refreshes my soul. He guides me along the right paths for his name's sake" (Psalm 23:2,3). See also 1 Corinthians 16:9.

HOW GOD GUIDES - contd.

(7) Supernatural Guidance.

(a) Dreams – God speaks to believers and unbelievers through dreams.

Unbelievers: Pharaoh & Nebuchadnezzar

Believers: Josephs in the OT and NT using dreams.

"For God does speak—now one way, now another—though no one perceives it. In a dream, in a vision of the night, when deep sleep falls on people as they slumber in their beds, he may speak in their ears and terrify them with warnings" (Job 33:14-16).

HOW GOD GUIDES - contd.

(b) Signs: These are to confirm God's will. An example is putting out a fleece by Gideon (Judges 6:36-40).

After Samuel anointed Saul as the first king of Israel, he gave Saul three signs to confirm God's will (1 Samuel 10:1-7).

The star guided the wise men from the East when they visited the baby Jesus (Matthew 2:1,9,10).

On the I-95, we may see South 30 miles to Miami – The sign indicates you are in the right direction

HOW GOD GUIDES - contd.

(3) Visions: God spoke to Abraham and Jacob in visions (Genesis 15:1; 46:2)

Ezekiel said, "I was among the exiles by the Kebar River, the heavens were opened and I saw visions of God" (Ezekiel 1:1).

God revealed Nebuchadnezzar's dream to Daniel:

"During the night the mystery was revealed to Daniel in a vision. Then Daniel praised the God of heaven" (Daniel 2:19).

HOW GOD GUIDES - contd.

(4) **Voice:** God sometimes directly speaks to people.

"Then the LORD spoke to you out of the fire. You heard the sound of words but saw no form; there was only a voice" (Deuteronomy 4:12)

"A voice from the cloud said, 'This is my Son, whom I love; with him I am well pleased. Listen to him!'" (Matthew 17:5).

A voice instructed Peter (Acts 10:13; 11:7).

HOW GOD GUIDES - contd.

(5) Angels: They appear in human form and guide. They help, serve, and minister to the saints.

An angel told Hagar, "Go back to your mistress and submit to her" (Genesis 16:9). See also Genesis 16:11.

The angel appeared to Jacob in the dream (Genesis 31:11).

Paul said, "Last night an angel of the God to whom I belong and whom I serve stood beside me" (Acts 27:23).

HOW GOD GUIDES - contd.

(6) **Spiritual Gifts:** God reveals His will through spiritual gifts (1 Corinthians 12:8-10):

- Wisdom
- Knowledge
- Faith
- Healing
- Miraculous powers
- Prophecy
- Discernment of spirits
- Speaking in different kinds of tongues
- Interpretation of tongues

HOW GOD GUIDES - contd.

(7) **Prophecy:** This is the major spiritual gift God uses to reveal His will. The large part of the OT is in form of prophecy.

Prophets are major vessels in the church (Ephesians 4:11).

The prophets in Antioch set Paul and Barnabas apart for the missionary work (Acts 13:1-3).

"In the past God spoke to our ancestors through the prophets at many times and in various ways, but in these last days he has spoken to us by his Son, whom he appointed heir of all things" (Hebrews 1:1-2).

CONCLUSION

1. CAUTION: Satan too can use the supernatural means of guidance, e.g. false prophets.

2. In summary, there are at least 6 natural ways and 7 supernatural ways God guides.

3. The 3 most important forms of guidance are God's Word, the Holy Spirit, and circumstances.

4. Two or three witness or combinations of these forms of guidance should be enough.

5. God uses the umpire of peace (Colossians 3:15) to settle/confirm issues.

6. We should pray like Jesus: "Not my will, but yours be done" (Luke 22:42).

QUESTIONS

REFERENCES

M. N. O. Sadiku, *How to Discover God's Will for Your Life*. Philadelphia, PA: Covenant Publishers, 1991.

CHAPTER 6
ALL THINGS ARE COMMITTED TO JESUS - PART 1

Presented by:

Matthew N. O. Sadiku
Website: www.matthew-sadiku.com
Email: sadiku@ieee.org

CLASSIFICAITON OF SERMONS

Sermons can be classified as follows:

- Encouragement
- Comfort
- Correction
- Inspiration
- Evangelism
- Teaching/Knowledge

This sermon is on the knowledge of Christ.

INTRODUCTION

"The Father loves the Son and has COMMITTED ALL THINGS into his hands" (John 3:35, emphasis mine).

What the Father has committed to His Son includes salvation, forgiveness, healing, authority, judgment, etc.

We will consider seven of them in this sermon and the remaining seven in the next.

1. SALVATION

Salvation is the greatest need of mankind.

Salvation is ultimately a gift from God through what Jesus Christ has done on the cross.

Jesus is the only way to heaven. No one, regardless of economic status, or personal holiness, can come to God the Father except through Jesus.

This is what Jesus Himself claimed: "I am the way, the truth, and the life. No one can come to the Father except through me" (John 14:6, NLT).

SALVATION - contd.

The apostles of Jesus echoed the same thing: "There is salvation in no one else! God has given no other name under heaven by which we must be saved" (Acts 4:12).

Illustration: A college student said all religions say the same thing. This is erroneous because no other religious leader claims that he is the way to God.

If we can save ourselves through works of righteousness, Christ died for nothing (Galatians 2:21).

2. FORGIVENESS

The power and authority to forgive sins has been given to Jesus Christ because He is the divine Son, He is God in the flesh, Immanuel.

No one (pope, priests, pastors, etc.) has the authority or power to forgive sins.

Only Jesus can forgive sin.

Jesus did only what only God could do – forgive sin

Jesus showed the religious leaders that He had the authority on earth to forgive sins. He said:

"So I will prove to you that the Son of Man[a] has the authority on earth to forgive sins" (Mark 2:10).

FORGIVENESS - contd.

Jesus forgave before He healed.

Jesus forgave the paralyzed man (Luke 5:20). Jesus forgave the adulterous woman (John 8:11). Jesus gave us too the power to give sins.

"If you forgive anyone's sins, they are forgiven. If you do not forgive them, they are not forgiven" (John 20:23).

We too must forgive. "If you do not forgive others their sins, your Father will not forgive your sins" (Matthew 6:14-15 KJV).

3. HEALING

The power and authority to heal has been committed to Jesus by the Father.

The healing power comes from Jesus Christ, the great physician.

He is the Sun of Righteousness who came with healing in his wings.

There is Power in the Name of Jesus. The devil trembles when he hears the Name of Jesus.

We are told that: "God anointed Jesus of Nazareth with the Holy Spirit and with power. He went about doing good and healing all who were oppressed by the devil, for God was with him" (Acts 10:38, ESV).

HEALING - contd.

Jesus healed everyone who came to Him, regardless of their disease.

"News about him spread as far as Syria, and people soon began bringing to him all who were sick. And whatever their sickness or disease, or if they were demon possessed or epileptic or paralyzed—he healed them all" (Matthew 4:24).

Jesus is still in the business of healing and He has not changed. He still heals today and around the world. "Jesus Christ is the same yesterday, today, and forever" (Hebrews 13:8).

4. ACCESS TO GOD

God has made His son, Jesus Christ, the great high priest, to be the only way to Him.

Jesus said: "I am the way, and the truth, and the life; no one comes to the Father but through Me" (John 14:6).

"Through him we have also obtained access by faith into this grace in which we stand, and we rejoice in hope of the glory of God" (Romans 5:2).

In the Old Testament, there was distance between God and His people. Only the high priest could enter His presence, and then only once a year (Hebrews 9:7).

ACCESS TO GOD - contd.

Under the new covenant, the entire world, all people, of all races, have direct access to God through Jesus Christ.

It is an immense privilege of having access to God through the son, Jesus Christ (John 14:6).

Jesus is the only way to the Father. He is our direct access. No middleman is necessary.

"For through him we both have access to the Father by one Spirit" (Ephesians 2:18).

5. MEDIATION

Mediation has to do with establishing and maintaining some kind of relationship between God and man.

A mediator is someone who reconciles conflict in a relationship.

The ministry of mediation has been committed to Jesus Christ. He is the mediator between God and mankind. "For this reason Christ is the mediator of a new covenant, that those who are called may receive the promised eternal inheritance" (Hebrews 9:15).

God is holy, while man is unholy. Therefore, man has not been able to approach God without going through a mediator.

MEDIATION - contd.

Moses is regarded as the mediator of the old covenant, while Jesus is the mediator of the new covenant (Deuteronomy 5:5, Hebrews 12:24).

"For *there is* one God and one Mediator between God and men, *the* Man Christ Jesus" (1 Timothy 2:5).

Jesus is the perfect bridge between God and human beings because He is both truly God and truly man.

Due to Jesus' mediation, we have peace with God and we have access to God.

6. ADVOCACY

An advocate is someone who pleads another person's case by defending him.

Jesus is our Advocate with the Father, interceding in heaven for Christians who sin on earth. He is our Advocate in the heavenly court.

"My dear children, I write this to you so that you will not sin. But if anybody does sin, we have an advocate with the Father—Jesus Christ, the Righteous One" (1 John 2:1).

Jesus Christ has been called to stand at our side and be our ultimate lawyer. He appeals to the Father on our behalf.

ADVOCACY - contd.

Jesus is our Advocate in heaven (Job 16:19. NLT), while the Holy is our Advocate residing in us (John 14:26, 15:26).

Right now, Jesus is pleading with the Father on our behalf, interceding for us that we might be forgiven, purified, and empowered to live a holy life.

Jesus pleads our case before the Father, the Righteous Judge, and against Satan the accuser of the brethren.

7. JUDGMENT

Judgment is the process by which man is held responsible and accountable for his behavior.

God has committed judgment to His Son, Jesus Christ.

"For the Father judges no one, but has committed all judgment to the Son. Most assuredly, I say to you, he who hears My word and believes in Him who sent Me has everlasting life, and shall not come into judgment, but has passed from death into life… has given Him authority to execute judgment also, because He is the Son of Man" (John 5:22,24,27, NKJV).

God is the Supreme Judge of the world. Since God is both holy and just, He must judge evil and vindicate those who have been wronged.

JUDGMENT - contd.

God will judge the world; but only through His Son, whom he has appointed to carry out the business of judgment.

Judgment is the prerogative of divinity. Jesus alone has authority to judge.

As judge, Jesus has the authority and the power to forgive sins.

Jesus will act as a fair judge of the living and the dead at the end of time.

CONCLUSION

"All things have been committed to me by my Father. No one knows who the Son is except the Father, and no one knows who the Father is except the Son and those to whom the Son chooses to reveal him" (Luke 10:22).

God has committed all things to His Son, Jesus.

For this reason, Jesus Christ has many names and titles: Son of Man, Emmanuel, Messiah, Prince of Peace, Alpha and Omega, Light of the world, King of kings, Lord of Lords, the Creator of the universe, etc.

These and other titles show His unique and perfect role as God.

With this head-and-heart knowledge of Jesus, we should go into the world and share Jesus with others who are still living in rebellion.

THANK YOU!

REFERENCES

M. N. O. Sadiku, *All Things Committed to Jesus.* Bloomington, IN: iUniverse, 2021.

CHAPTER 7
ALL THINGS ARE COMMITTED TO JESUS - PART 2

Presented by:

Matthew N. O. Sadiku
Website: www.matthew-sadiku.com
Email: sadiku@ieee.org

INTRODUCTION

This is a continuation of the previous sermon.

"The Father loves the Son and has committed all things into his hands" (John 3:35).

This is one of the all-things verses in the New Testament.

All things work together (Romans 8:28)

INTRODUCTION - contd.

I can do all things through Christ (Phil. 4:13)

All things are possible with God (Mark 10:27)

All things are possible with him who believes (Mark 9:23)

All things are put under Jesus power (John 13:3)

The Spirit searches all things (1 Corinthians 2:10)

God has put all things under His feet (Ephesians 2:22)

God graciously give us all things (Romans 8:32)

SUMMARY OF LAST SERMON

1. Salvation

2. Forgiveness

3. Healing

4. Access to God

5. Mediation

6. Advocacy

7. Judgment

8. NAMES ABOVE ALL NAMES

The Father has given His Son, Jesus Christ, the name above all names and the highest seat of honor.

The Name of Jesus is higher than any other name.

It is the most powerful name.

"**Therefore God exalted him to the highest place and gave him the name that is above every name, that at the name of Jesus every knee should bow, in heaven and on earth and under the earth** (Philippians 2:9,10 KJV).

The name of Jesus is a key for us to receive from God.

NAMES ABOVE ALL NAMES - contd.

Jesus said that whatever we ask the Father in His name, He will do it (John 14:13,14).

Believers are expected to believe and use the name of Jesus (1 John 3:23 KJV).

"And these signs will accompany those who believe: In my name they will drive out demons; they will speak in new tongues" (Mark 16:17).

9. THE ONE WITH ALL AUTHORITY

After the crucifixion, God the Father officially took back all authority in heaven, on earth, and under the earth and gave it to His Son Jesus.

Jesus said to His apostle, "All authority in heaven and on earth has been given to me" (Matthew 28:18, ESV).

People who have authorities set the rules, determine the judgments, and make the verdicts.

Jesus has the AUTHORITY OVER ALL: Satan, all demons, over all angels, all things, sins, life, death, etc.

Jesus has delegated that authority to us.

10. THE GOOD SHEPHERD

God has committed the task of shepherding over His flock to Jesus Christ, like David.

Jesus is the Good Shepherd:

"I am the good shepherd. The good shepherd lays down his life for the sheep. "I am the good shepherd; I know my sheep and my sheep know me" (John 10:11,14).

Jesus is our indwelling Shepherd, caring for us His flock both inwardly and outwardly.

Jesus provides and protects the sheep.

THE GOOD SHEPHERD - contd.

Jesus is a good Shepherd who gives us abundant life and leads us to green pasture.

Jesus is the Great Shepherd:

"Now may the God of peace, who through the blood of the eternal covenant brought back from the dead our Lord Jesus, that great Shepherd of the sheep" (Hebrews 13:20).

Jesus is the Chief Shepherd:

"When the Chief Shepherd appears, you will receive the crown of glory that will never fade away" (1 Peter 5:4).

11. THE LIGHT OF THE WORLD

Jesus said, "I am the light of the world. Whoever follows me will never walk in darkness, but will have the light of life" (John 8:12, KJV).

Jesus, the life-giving glory of God, is present in every believer. Jesus is the light and life of God shining in the darkness.

Our world, our nation, men and woman, young and old are enslaved by darkness. They gamble with life and make a lot of mistakes. They walk in the dark and are confused. They do not know what they are doing.

They need Jesus' light.

LIGHT OF THE WORLD - contd.

"Anyone who hates a brother or sister is in the darkness and walks around in the darkness. They do not know where they are going, because the darkness has blinded them" (1 John 2:11).

Jesus invites us to shine His light into the world around us (Matthew 5:14-16). In His light, we see light (Psalm 36:9).

When we dwell in the light, we do not stumble.

The Word of God is the light. We should let it dwell in us richly (Colossians 3:16).

"Your word is a lamp for my feet, a light on my path" (Psalm 119:105).

12. THE GLORY OF GOD

The word "glory" refers to God's intense, profound presence.

Jesus is the glory of God.

The Word became flesh and made his dwelling among us. We have seen his glory, the glory of the one and only Son, who came from the Father, full of grace and truth.

"God's Son shines out with God's glory, and all that God's Son is and does marks him as God" (Hebrews 1:3, TLB).

The OT saints experienced God's glory, shekinah, which was the visible manifestation of the invisible God. Pillar of cloud in the morning & pillar of fire at the evening.

THE GLORY OF GOD - contd.

Our chief business on earth is to glorify the glorious One and live for the glory of God.

"As all of us reflect the Lord's glory with faces that are not covered with veils, we are being changed into his image with ever-increasing glory. This comes from the Lord, who is the Spirit" (2 Corinthians 3:18, GW).

When we walk in righteousness, the glory of God shines in our life.

We are to carry that glory with us wherever we go.

13. THE KING OF KINGS

The Bible is a book about a King and a Kingdom.

It describes Jesus as the King of kings, Lord of Lords, etc.

Jesus came to this world to establish a spiritual kingdom.

Jesus said, "So as my Father has given me a kingdom, I'm giving it to you" (Luke 22:29, GW).

Jesus' role is described as Prophet, Priest, and King. He is King of heaven and earth, of the Universe.

We have been translated from the kingdom of darkness into the kingdom of God's dear Son.

"You are a chosen people, a royal priesthood, a holy nation, God's special possession" (1 Peter 2:9).

THE KING OF KINGS - contd.

We should live by the kingdom principles.

We should be kingdom conscious in our thinking and behavior.

Our citizenship is in heaven, and from it we await a Savior. We are saints at West Palm Beach in Christ (Colossians 1:2).

"Seek first his kingdom and his righteousness, and all these things will be given to you as well" (Mt. 6:33).

"Seek the Kingdom of God above all else, and he will give you everything you need" (Luke 12:31, NLT).

14. THE HEIR OF ALL THINGS

God the Father has appointed His Son Jesus to inherit all things (Hebrews 1:3, KJV).

"In these last days he has spoken to us by his Son, whom he appointed heir of all things, and through whom also he made the universe" (Hebrew 1:2).

As adopted children of God, we are joint heirs with Christ.

"The Spirit himself testifies with our spirit that we are God's children. Now if we are children, then we are heirs—heirs of God and co-heirs with Christ, if indeed we share in his sufferings in order that we may also share in his glory" (Romans 8:16,17).

HEIR OF ALL THINGS - contd.

"Because you are his sons, God sent the Spirit of his Son into our hearts, the Spirit who calls out, "*Abba*, Father." So you are no longer a slave, but God's child; and since you are his child, God has made you also an heir" (Galatians 4:6,7).

"Dear friends, now we are children of God, and what we will be has not yet been made known. But we know that when Christ appears, we shall be like him, for we shall see him as he is. All who have this hope in him purify themselves, just as he is pure" (1 John 3:2,3).

Complete obedience, faithfulness, and holiness merit joint- heirship with Christ.

Start seeing yourself, as a joint heir with Jesus! There is a rich inheritance and eternal glory awaiting you.

CONCLUSION

"All things have been committed to me by my Father. No one knows who the Son is except the Father, and no one knows who the Father is except the Son and those to whom the Son chooses to reveal him" (Luke 10:22).

God has committed all things to His Son, Jesus.

You can accomplish great things through Jesus -- Name Above All Names.

Jesus speaks from God and for God and as God.

With this head-and-heart knowledge of Jesus:

(1) You should make Jesus your Savior and Lord if you have not done so.

CONCLUSION - contd.

(2) We should give Jesus the rightful place in our life.

(3) We should have confidence in Jesus power, wisdom, healing, etc.

(4) We should go into the world and share Jesus with others who are still living in rebellion.

(5) We should walk with the King and be a blessing.

THANK YOU!

REFERENCES

M. N. O. Sadiku, *All Things Committed to Jesus.* Bloomington, IN: iUniverse, 2021.

CHAPTER 8
KEYS TO EFFECTIVE LEADERSHIP (AND SERVICE IN THE KINGDOM)

Presented by:

Matthew N. O. Sadiku
Web: www.matthew-sadiku.com
Email: sadiku@ieee.org

INTRODUCTION

Leadership is critical to our everyday lives.

A good leader is required for a group to achieve success.

Leadership can be used to create positive situations and experiences wherever you are.

Everything rises or falls with leaders.

We need leaders at work, at home, at church, among colleagues or friends, in the society, etc.

Good leaders are hard to find in all these areas.

WHAT IS LEADERSHIP?

A leader is the one who leads.

As a leader, you need to know the way, show the way, and lead the way.

You must have a destination/vision and know how to get there.

Leadership may be regarded as the process of leading followers.

Leaders are needed everywhere including churches and homes.

Leadership is now regarded as an art and something to be learned over time.

We all have leadership potential but great and effective leaders have high potentials than the rest of us.

A leader can mislead others and are responsible to God.

LEADERSHIP STYLES

Leadership styles and behaviors have direct impact on a group's productivity and satisfaction.

There are different types of leadership, as shown below.

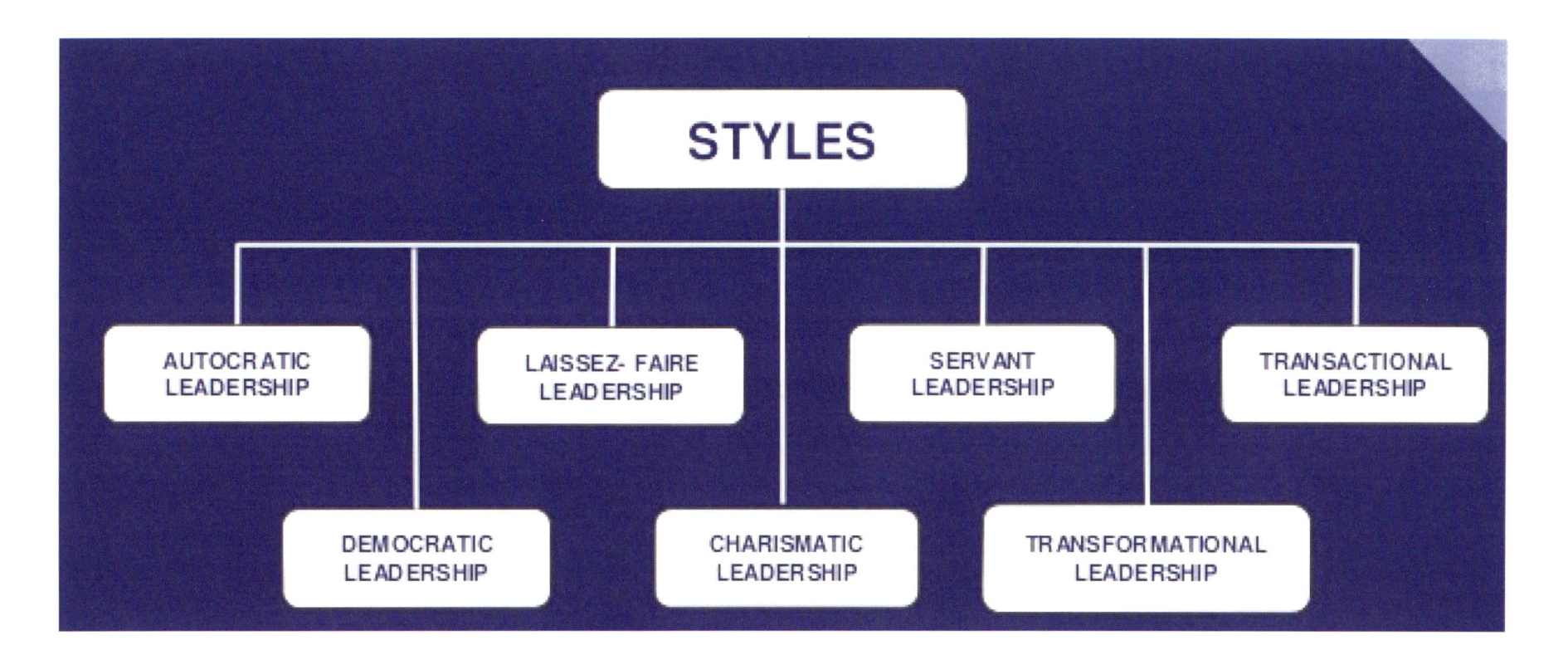

```
                          STYLES
    ┌──────────┬────────────┬────────────┬──────────┐
AUTOCRATIC   LAISSEZ-FAIRE   SERVANT      TRANSACTIONAL
LEADERSHIP   LEADERSHIP      LEADERSHIP   LEADERSHIP

         DEMOCRATIC    CHARISMATIC    TRANSFORMATIONAL
         LEADERSHIP    LEADERSHIP     LEADERSHIP
```

5 POPULAR LEADERSHIP STYLES

1. **Transformational leaders** are visionary, charismatic, self- aware, and confident.

2. **Transactional leadership** is the leadership style where leaders focus on the day-to-day tasks or transactions and reward subordinates for tasks.

3. **Charismatic leadership** refers to the ability to inspire others with their personality and vision.

4. **Pastoral Leadership** involves leading with a pastoral heart.

5. **Servant leadership** is based on serving the needs of others. It is a concept that Jesus demonstrated to His disciples (Mark 10:45). It is leading like Jesus, as shown next.

LEADERSHIP STYLES - contd.

Jesus said, "The Son of Man did not come to be served, but to serve, and to give his life as a ransom for many" (Matthew 20:28). "The greatest among you shall be your servant. Whoever exalts himself will be humbled, and whoever humbles himself will be exalted." (Mt. 23:11-12).

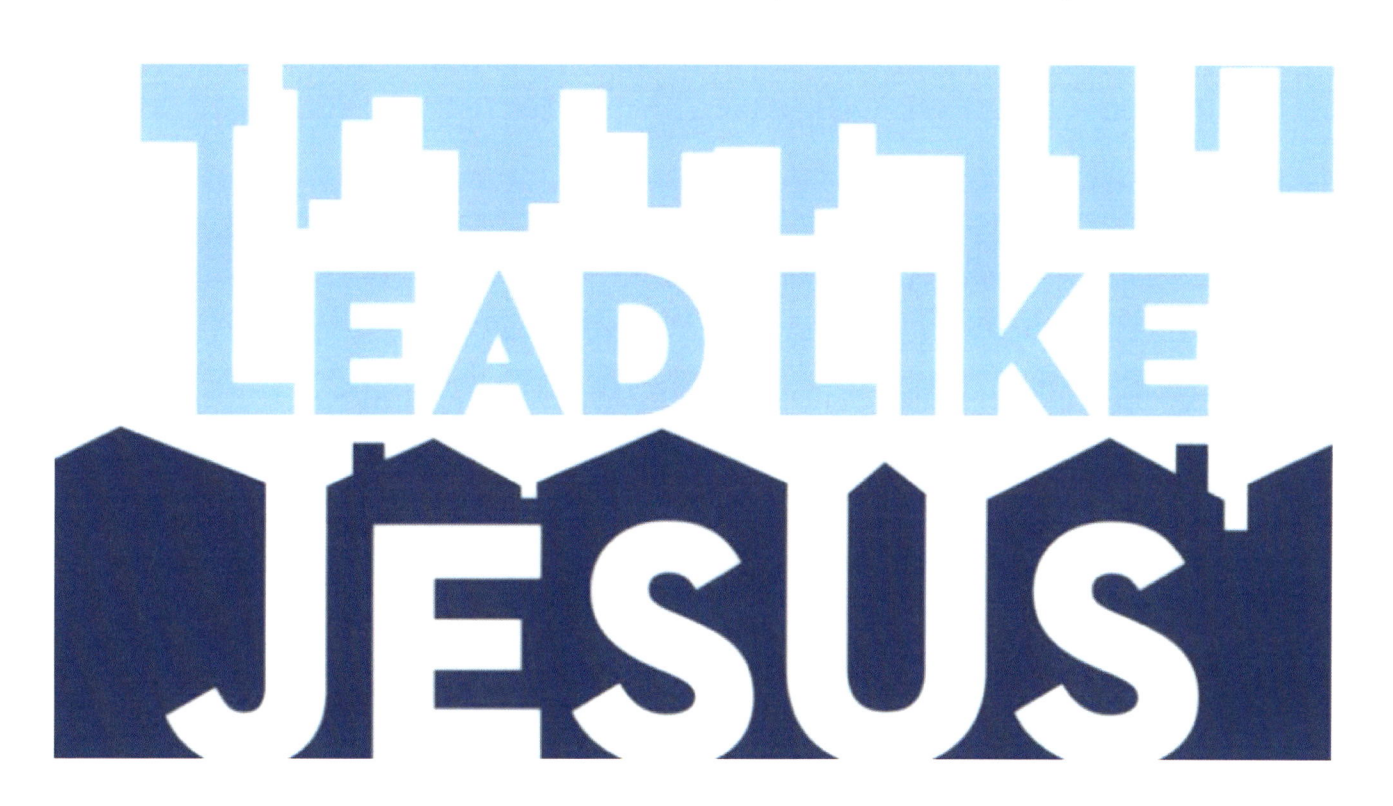

CHARACTERISTICS OF A LEADER

1. *Faith:* Faith is the first and perhaps the most important mark of a Christian leader. It is seeing what others do not see.

   Faith is the ability to see the light at the end of the tunnel. It is faith that separates leaders from followers.

2. *Mission:* Same as vision or purpose. A mission is a vision that is acted upon. People with missions change our world. Every great accomplishment starts with someone burdened with a vision. Great leaders are driven by their vision, mission, or dream. Vision sees needs and finds ways to meet the needs, undaunted by the problems.

3. *Character:* You recognize a leader by his/her spiritual and moral integrity. David, the second king of Israel, is a good model of sound character. He was the yardstick by whom other kings were measured (1 Kings 3:3,6; 2 Kings 14:3; 22:2).

CHARACTERISTICS - contd.

4. *Competency:* An incompetent leader can hardly command loyal followers; e.g. Baptist pastors earn doctoral degree. Since leadership is getting things done, competence may mean being able to organize others, set goals, establish procedures, reward accomplishments, negotiate disputes, and take corrective measures.

5. *Compassion:* Lack of compassion for hurting people disqualifies one from leadership. Good leaders genuinely care for people. Our attitude to people's needs must be the same as that of Christ who went about doing good and having compassion on people.

CHARACTERISTICS - contd.

6. *Courage/Boldness:* This is being willing to take risks for the greater good. It takes courage to do what is right. Courage may mean being able to keep going when the burden is heavy and there is no end in sight.

7. *Knowledge:* Knowledge is the accumulation of facts. It is gained by diligent study. For those in leadership positions, mental stretching should be the way of life (2 Timothy 2:15, KJV). "Without knowledge, my people perish" (Hos. 4:6). Leader must know God, know about marriage, know about money management, and know about the people they are leading. A commitment to acquiring knowledge will make a leader sound and effective.

CHARACTERISTICS - contd.

8. *Effective Communication:* Communication is the transmission of an idea, instruction, opinion, or emotion from one person to another. A leader must be an effective communicator of their goals and plans to those they are leading.

The ability to communicate effectively with others could be one of the most valuable assets of a leader.

US President Gerald Ford said, "If I went back to college again, I'd concentrate on two areas: learning to write and to speak before an audience. Nothing in life is more important than the ability to communicate effectively."

WHAT IS EFFECTIVE LEADERSHIP?

An effective leader can lead people to the right destination.

Effective leadership is the ability to successfully influence a group of people.

Effective leaders communicate effectively, delegate work, encourage strategic thinking, and motivate others to do their best.

An effective Christian leader is one who is enabled by the Holy Spirit to help other believers follow their lead to higher morale and better outcomes.

An effective husband leads the family to a successful marriage.

KEYS TO EFFECTIVE LEADERSHIP

Followers naturally admire and respect the following ten qualities in an effective leader.

1. Living by Kingdom Principles

(a) Faith – To walk closely with God, we must walk by faith, not be sight (2 Cor. 5:7).

(b) Righteousness – This is doing what is right or just.

(c) Love – A leader must love God above all else and love other fellows (Matt. 22:37-40).

(d) Wisdom – A leader must make wise choices to gain the trust of followers.

(e) Humility – This is the quality of being respective of others. It manifests itself in our relationship toward God, toward ourselves, and toward others.

EFFECTIVE LEADERSHIP - contd.

Living by Kingdom Principles – contd.

(f) Unity – This enables a group to do exploit (Genesis 11:1-9).

(g) Influence – We are to influence the world as light and as salt.

(h) Giving – We should give to God (vertically) and others who are in need (horizontally).

(i) Prayer – This is what distinguishes a spiritual leader from a secular leader.

(j) Holy Spirit – A Christian leader must be empowered and led by the Holy Spirit.

(k) Lordship of Christ: A leader must submit to the lordship of Christ and avoid leading others astray.

EFFECTIVE LEADERSHIP - contd.

2. Fear of the Lord

This is the duty of every person (Ecclesiastes 12:13).

Fearing God is having deep respect for Him.

Without this, God is deleted in our quest.

If anything goes, then in the end everything goes and all becomes futile and meaningless.

The fear of God is a godly means of avoiding sin.

Joseph feared God and said, "How then could I do such a wicked thing and sin against God?" (Genesis 39:9)

David Oyedepo said, "He who fears God fares well."

EFFECTIVE LEADERSHIP - contd.

Fear of the Lord – contd.

"The fear of the LORD is the beginning of knowledge, but fools despise wisdom and instruction" (Proverbs 1:7).

"Do not be wise in your own eyes; fear the LORD and shun evil" (Proverbs 3:7).

"Where is the man who fears the Lord? God will teach him how to choose the best. He shall live within God's circle of blessing, and his children shall inherit the earth. Friendship with God is reserved for those who reverence him. With them alone he shares the secrets of his promises" (Psalm 25:12-14, TLB).

EFFECTIVE LEADERSHIP - contd.

3. Integrity

This is the moral dimension that separates wisdom from intelligence, learning, and cleverness.

Integrity makes us do the right thing.

Solomon said, "I would have you learn this great fact: that a life of doing right is the wisest life there is. If you live that kind of life, you'll not limp or stumble as you run" (Proverbs 4:11,12, TLB).

"The integrity of the upright shall guide them" (Proverbs 11:3).

EFFECTIVE LEADERSHIP - contd.

Integrity – contd.

"A good name is better than fine perfume" (Ecclesiastes 7:1).

David said to Araunah: "No, I insist on paying you for it. I will not sacrifice to the LORD my God burnt offerings that cost me nothing" (2 Samuel 24:24).

Adversity or trouble is the negative test of integrity. Prosperity is its positive test.

EFFECTIVE LEADERSHIP - contd.

4. Faithfulness

This is being able to keep your word or promise or commitment.

A faithful leader is true to his word.

Faithfulness is crucial to lasting relationships.

Every sin may be considered unfaithfulness, e.g. Saul & Israel (1 Chronicles 5:25; 9:1; 10:13; Ezekiel 15:8; 39:23).

Trust is a by-product of faithfulness.

Proverbs 3:3 urges us to cherish love and faithfulness.

EFFECTIVE LEADERSHIP - contd.

Faithfulness – contd.

God likes faithful people and so do men and women.

God wants us to be faithful in paying our tithes and offering. He wants us to be faithful to our spouse, our fellow believers, our employer, our co-workers, our friends, etc.

"Many a man proclaims his own loyalty, but A FAITHFUL MAN WHO CAN FIND?" (Proverbs 20:6, emphasis mine).

EFFECTIVE LEADERSHIP - contd.

5. Unselfishness

This is putting yourself second and prioritizing the needs of others before your own.

Love does not insist on its own way. Love is not selfish.

"We who are strong ought to bear with the failings of the weak and not to please ourselves" (Romans 15:1).

"Let nothing be done through selfish ambition or conceit, but in lowliness of mind let each esteem others better than himself. Let each of you look out not only for his own interests, but also for the interests of others" (Philippians 2:3,4, NKJV).

EFFECTIVE LEADERSHIP - contd.

Unselfishness - contd.

Jesus demonstrated selflessness by choosing the way of the cross.

As we develop the mindset of Christ, we become unselfish like Him.

David refused to drink the water brought by men who risked their life (2 Samuel 23:15-17).

EFFECTIVE LEADERSHIP - contd.

6. Discipline

Discipline or self-control is important in leadership.

It is the ability to rule oneself - body and spirit.

It is being able to master, control, curb, or retrain one's desires.

"For God gave us a spirit not of fear but of power and love and self-control" (2 Tim. 1:7).

We must apply self-discipline in our body (mouth, eyes and feet), heart, and speech.

EFFECTIVE LEADERSHIP - contd.

Discipline – contd.

"Every athlete exercises self-control in all things" (1 Corinthians 9:25).

It is lack of discipline to have sex outside marriage.

"The way of the faithless is their ruin" (Proverbs 13:15).

"Sensible people control their temper; they earn respect by overlooking wrongs" (Prov. 19:11).

Job said, "I made a covenant with my eyes not to look lustfully at a young woman" (Job 31:1).

EFFECTIVE LEADERSHIP - contd.

7. Focus

F.O.C.U.S means Follow One Course Until Successful.

Focus is the ability to concentrate and keep the main thing the main thing.

Effective leaders are focused on their mission.

Being focused helps you to be more productive.

Avoid multitasking, prioritize your tasks, focus on what you do best, and let go of the rest.

EFFECTIVE LEADERSHIP - contd.

Focus – contd.

Paul is a one-thing man. He said, "This one thing I do, forgetting those things which are behind, and reaching forth unto those things which are before" (Philippians 3:13).

Jesus said we should seek first His kingdom (Matthew 6:33).

EFFECTIVE LEADERSHIP - contd.

8. Servant Heart

Many leaders in the Bible are called the servant of God.

God told Joshua, "My servant Moses is dead (Joshua 1:2)

David was God's servant (2 Samuel 7:8)

God asked the devil, "Have you seen my servant Job" (Job 1:8)

Elijah, Isaiah, Peter, etc. were God's servants

Jesus was a servant leader (Mark 10:45).

EFFECTIVE LEADERSHIP - contd.

9. Effective time management

This is planning how to efficiently use and deliberately control the time you spend to maximize productivity, efficiency, and success.

Peter Drucker said, "Until we can manage time, we can manage nothing."

Common time management mistakes include overcommitment, refusing to delegate, procrastination, or overextending while attempting to multitask.

Instead of trying to tackle everything at once, prioritize and do the most important, not the most urgent.

You cannot do it all. Delegate things to capable disciples.

EFFECTIVE LEADERSHIP - contd.

Effective time management - contd.

Moses learned to delegate responsibilities to some capable, honest men who fear God (Exodus 18:17-26).

Jesus appointed 12 apostles and gave them authority to do things on His behalf. Time management skills are shown in the figure below.

Using Free Time Smartly: Time to relax, but you need to be productive with your free time, too — 01

Prioritizing: Always more to do than time, so we have to prioritize — 02

Delegating & Outsourcing: Allow yourself to delegate the work that's not a top priority — 03

Goal Setting: You can't reach a destination if you don't know where you are going — 04

Planning & Scheduling: Saves time & boosts productivity — 05

Learn to Say No: Set boundaries and respect your time and plans — 06

Self-Discipline: Learning & practicing self-discipline is a life-long process — 07

Source: "Time management skills," https://www.sketchbubble.com/en/presentation-time-management-skills.html

EFFECTIVE LEADERSHIP - contd.

10. Patience

It takes time to mature and we must be patient with each other.

Be patient with what can be changed and accept what cannot.

A mature person bears the fruit of the Spirit which includes patience.

Love is patient. Love can wait (1 Corinthians 13:4).

We should all carry on our back a sign reading:

> PLEASE BE PATIENT WITH ME
> I'M UNDER CONSTRUCTION
> GOD IS NOT FINISHED WITH ME

Paul said, "We urge you, brothers, admonish the idle, encourage the fainthearted, help the weak, BE PATIENT WITH THEM ALL" (Thess. 5:14, ESV, emphasis mine; 2 Tim. 2:24).

DAVID – A MODEL OF EFFECTIVE LEADERSHIP

David feared the Lord and kept himself from iniquity (2 Samuel 22:24)

He was obedient to the Lord's commandments (1 Kings 15:5)

He sought God's approval in taking actions (1 Samuel 1:3,4.11,12)

His reaction to Saul, his enemy, was positive (1 Samuel 30:23, 2 Samuel 1). He was guided by integrity (2 Samuel 24).

"David shepherded them with integrity of heart; with skillful hands he led them" (Psalm 78:72).

The Lord was with him and he never lost a battle.

PAUL'S MODEL OF EFFECTIVE LEADERSHIP

"If someone aspires to be a church leader, he desires an honorable position.

So a church leader must be a man whose life is above reproach.

He must be faithful to his wife.

He must exercise self-control, live wisely, and have a good reputation.

He must enjoy having guests in his home,

and he must be able to teach. (1 Timothy 3:1,2).

PAUL'S MODEL - contd.

He must not be a heavy drinker or be violent.

He must be gentle, not quarrelsome, and not love money.

He must manage his own family well, having children who respect and obey him.

For if a man cannot manage his own household, how can he take care of God's church?" (1 Timothy 3:3-5).

CONCLUSION

Leaders are important people. They set the tone for a group or organization.

Everyone has a measure of leadership potential but the measure varies from person to person.

Followers naturally admire and respect a leader with the following five qualities: Faith, Mission, Character, Competence, and Compassion.

An effective leader is effective in managing people, resources, and time.

Evaluate your life in the light of these qualities of leadership.

To rise to the challenge of being a leader is a lifelong commitment.

QUESTIONS?

REFERENCES

M. N. O. Sadiku, *Wisdom: Your Key to Success.* Houston, TX: Covenant Publishers, 2009, chapter 19.

CHAPTER 9
TIME MANAGEMENT

Presented by:

Matthew N. O. Sadiku
Web: www.matthew-sadiku.com
Email: sadiku@ieee.org

WHAT IS TIME MANAGEMENT?

Time is perhaps the most precious thing in the world.

There are 24 hours a day and 168 hours in every week. How are you spending yours?

Simply, time management (TM) is the process of dividing your time between different activities.

It is making the most of your time and energy.

It is management of time in order to make the most out of it.

Failing to manage your time or poor time management can result in:
(1) Missed deadlines, (2) Poor work quality, (3) Unwanted stress, (4) Poor professional reputation, (4) Work and life imbalance

TM - contd.

Time management makes the difference between the wise and the foolish.

It makes the difference between the rich and the poor.

"Time, like money, is measured by our deeds" – George Eliot

Time is the great equalizer – everybody gets the same 24 hours a day.

"Time wasted is existence; used, it is life" – Edward Young

Wasting time is worse than wasting money.

TIME

Quotes About Time

- Good things come to those who wait
- Time heals all wounds
- There is no time like the present
- There is no time to loose
- Killing time
- Time is what you make of it
- Until we can manage time, we can manage nothing else – Peter Drucker

MANAGING TIME

Managing Time

There are 168 hours in every week.
How are you spending yours?

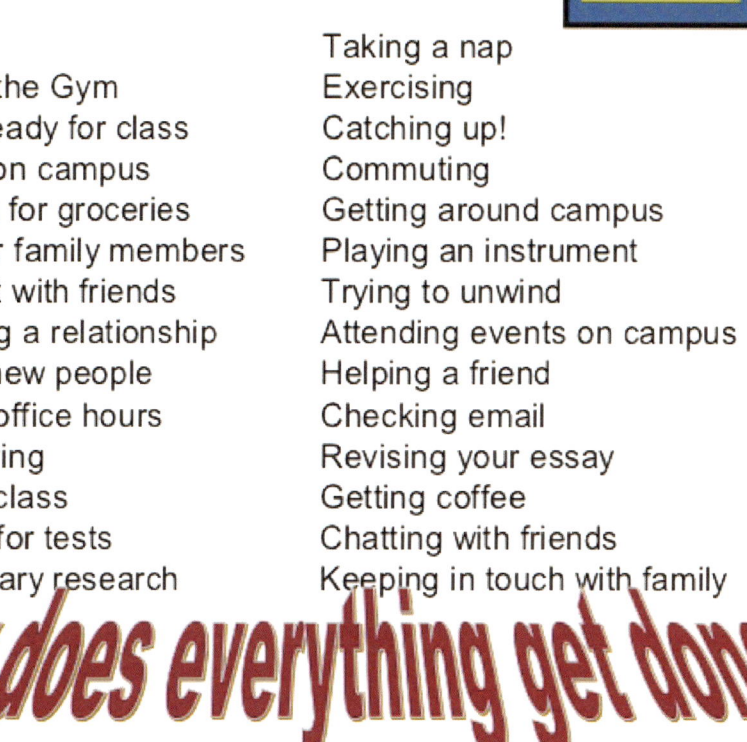

Sleeping	Taking a nap
Going to the Gym	Exercising
Getting ready for class	Catching up!
Working on campus	Commuting
Shopping for groceries	Getting around campus
Caring for family members	Playing an instrument
Going out with friends	Trying to unwind
Cultivating a relationship	Attending events on campus
Meeting new people	Helping a friend
Going to office hours	Checking email
Volunteering	Revising your essay
Going to class	Getting coffee
Studying for tests	Chatting with friends
Doing library research	Keeping in touch with family

How does everything get done?

191

WHY TIME MANAGEMENT?

Defining outcomes and physical actions required is the core process required to manage what you do.

Most of the time we struggle to create a balance between:

(1) Our Needs - eating, sleeping,

(2) Our Desires - Socializing, exercising, shopping, etc.

(3) Our Obligations – work, family, etc.

MYTHS ABOUT TIME MANAGEMENT

Time management is nothing but common sense. I do well in school, so I must be managing my time effectively.

It takes all the fun out of life.

Time management? I work better under pressure.

No matter what I do, I won't have enough time!

TIME MANAGEMENT IN ACADEMIA

You need to know the university's mission.

You need to know what is expected of you:

(1) Teaching, (2) Research/Funding, (3) Service

For promotion: Assistant Professor to Associate Professor to Full Professor.

From tenure track to tenured.

For doing research, use your graduate students.

Collaboration is very important for research and seeking funding.

TM FOR ACADEMICS - contd.

1. Don't overprepare or spend too long writing lectures.

2. Don't spend too long grading.

3. Set aside certain times of day to attend to emails.

4. Have a clear sense of your priorities.

5. Use diaries/wall planners/electronic versions.

6. Have goals for teaching, research, and service.

TIME MANAGEMENT IN INDUSTRY

You are responsible to your employer.

Know your company's mission.

Know your job expectation.

You are expected to deliver work on time.

Effective time management (TM) skills can have a positive impact on your work

TM is needed for more opportunities and career growth.

STEPS TO MANAGING YOUR TIME

1. Set Goals! Make your goals specific and concrete. Set both long-term goals and short-term ones to support them.

2. On daily basis, make a schedule, a To-Do List.

3. From your goals, set priorities. What's important and what isn't?

4. Plan to achieve your goals.

5. Block out a specific time to accomplish a task; e.g. Monday 1:00—2:00 Work on your dissertation

6. Study at the same time each day; make it a habit.

MANAGING YOUR TIME - contd.

7. Determine the time limits to achieve your goals.

8. Organize resources which are needed to execute a task to avoid delays.

9. Since a single individual cannot perform all the tasks single-handedly, delegation of work is necessary.

10. It is utmost important that the non-priority, redundant tasks are reduced.

11. Plan your time such as to create a stress-free working environment since stress leads to poor efficiency.

12. Planning tasks beforehand is crucial for effective time management.

SET PRIORITIES

Which goals are important to you? Which goals are urgent?

It is important to work on one task at a time.

Plan time to begin the process.

Faithfully using your student planner/calendar will help you to prioritize your work.

Know what works best for you: a planner, a calendar, an Outlook calendar, your cell phone, etc.

How can you establish priorities?

Use a "to-do list" – Cross off each task as you complete them.

PROCRASTINATION

Procrastination is delaying till tomorrow what you can do today. It is the thief of time and the archenemy of all students.

Forms of Procrastination:

(1) Ignoring the task, hoping it will go away

(2) Underestimating how long it will take

(3) Overestimating your abilities and resources

(4) Telling yourself that poor performance is okay

(5) Doing other things that are not important

(6) Talking about a hard job rather than doing it

(7) Becoming paralyzed when having to make choices

PROCRASTINATION - contd.

How to Overcome Procrastination:

(1) Win the mental battle by committing to being on time

(2) Set and keep deadlines

(3) Organize, schedule & plan

(4) Divide a big job into smaller ones

(5) Find a way to make fun of your work

(6) Reward yourself when you're done

(7) Don't let distractions sap your time

(8) Learn to say "No!" to low priority requests

(9) Just do it.

TIME WASTERS

Learn to recognize when you're wasting time.

Decide what you need to do and can realistically do.

Learn how to say "No" when you don't have time.

Use an answering machine and return calls at your convenience. The telephone is a major time killer.

Learn to say "I can't talk right now. I'll get back to you."

Ask yourself, "Do I really need to do this or not?"

IMPORTANCE AND URGENCY

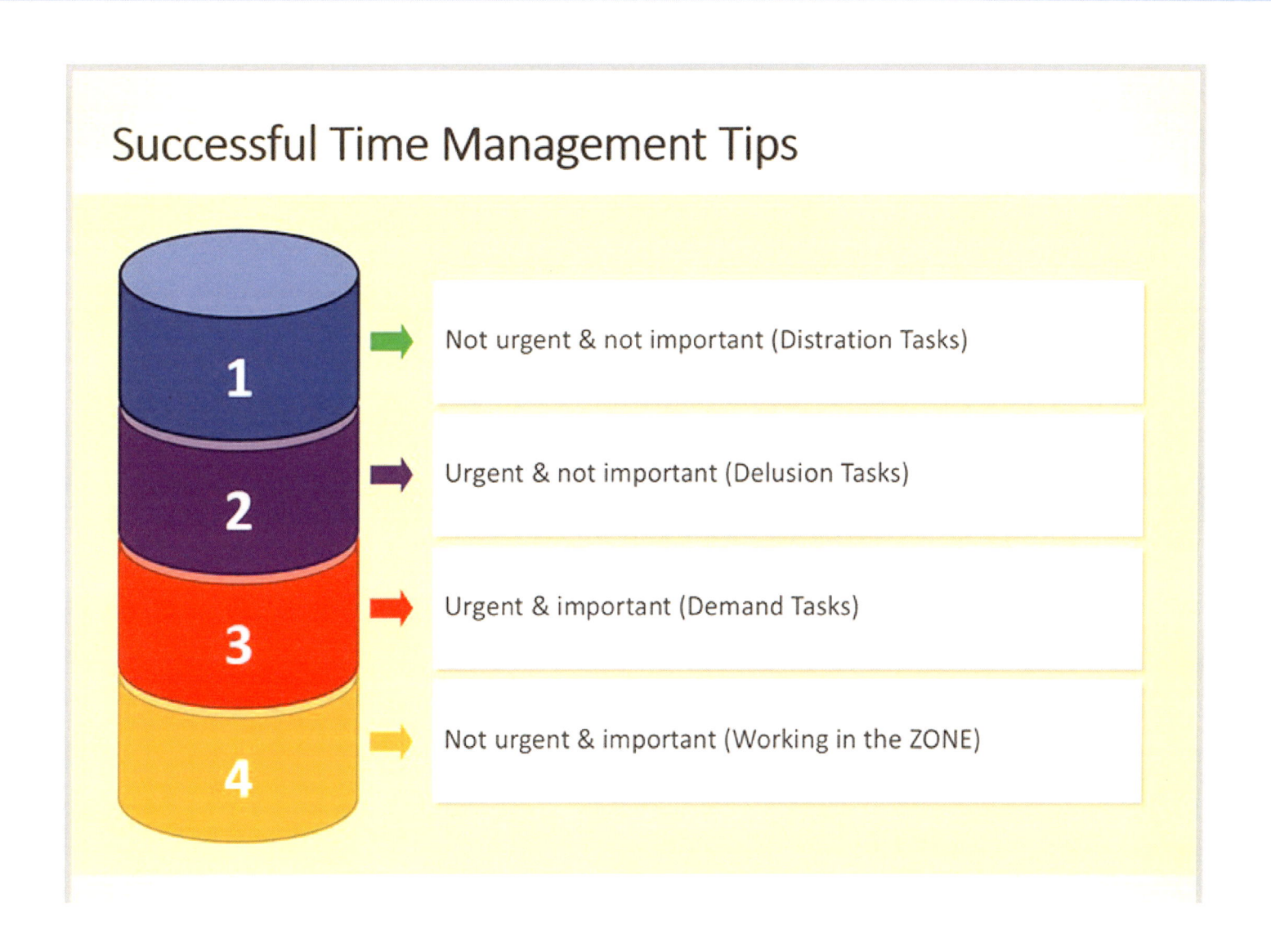

Successful Time Management Tips

1. → Not urgent & not important (Distration Tasks)
2. → Urgent & not important (Delusion Tasks)
3. → Urgent & important (Demand Tasks)
4. → Not urgent & important (Working in the ZONE)

ENERGY LEVEL

Energy level is important in time management.

Evaluate your energy level at different times of day.

Schedule tasks when you have the energy level to match.

If you are a "morning person," seize the early hours to study and do assignments that require focus.

If you are an "evening person," make sure that you are being productive and not sacrificing sleep for extra hours to socialize.

ARE YOU MAKING PROGRESS?

From time to time, revise your goals and plans.

- Are you paying attention to your schedule?
- Are you actually using your time wisely?
- Was your energy level appropriate?
- What changes need to be made to your weekly schedule?
- What are persistent time wasters?
- Was procrastination an issue?

Expect the unexpected.

ADVANTAGES/BENEFITS OF TIME MANAGEMENT

You are more productive.

You reduce your stress.

You achieve work-life balance.

You feel more confident in your ability to get things done.

You feel like you have more time in your day.

You achieve your goals.

Time management hones your leadership skills and reduces stress.

DISADVANTAGES OF TIME MANAGEMENT

You waste time in idle activities.

Poor TM may mean spending time on the wrong things.

Poor TM can lead to failure of all tasks.

Good TM skills take time to develop.

Creating a work-life balance can be complex.

Being too time-conscious can lead to mental and physical stress.

TM may take all the fun out of life.

CONCLUSION

Time and energy management can make you more productive and reduce your stress level.

The Three Steps: (1) Set goals, (2) Make a schedule, (3) Revisit and revise your plan.

Be tough with your time and prioritize.

Actively avoid procrastination and time wasters.

Learn to say "no" to distractions.

Employ a variety of time management strategies to maximize your time.

Relax and enjoy the extra time that you've discovered.

QUESTION?

REFERENCES

M. N. O. Sadiku, *Secrets of Conducting Research: In Engineering, Science, Humanities, and Social Sciences.* Ebookscrafter, 2023, chapter 8.

CHAPTER 10
STRESS MANAGEMENT

Presented by:

Matthew N. O. Sadiku
Web: www.matthew-sadiku.com
Email: sadiku@ieee.org

INTRODUCTION

Stress is our emotional and physical response to pressure.

Stress is the experience of being overwhelmed or unable to cope with pressure caused by outside events.

Everyone feels stress at times; it is a normal part of everyone's life.

We feel there are too many demands, and too few resources to cope.

STRESS MANAGEMENT

Stress management (SM) offers a range of strategies to help you better deal with stress and difficulty (adversity) in your life.

It includes practicing relaxation techniques such as deep breathing, yoga, meditation, exercise, and prayer.

It may seem like there's nothing you can do about stress. The bills won't stop coming, there will never be more hours in the day, and your work and family responsibilities will always be demanding.

TYPES OF STRESS

There are two types of stress:

1. Acute stress is the most common form of stress among humans worldwide. It lasts for a moment.

2. Chronic stress lasts for longer time spans. It can become a very serious health risk if it continues over a long period of time.

CATEGORIES OF STRESS

(1) Emotional stress

(2) Financial stress – misuse of credit card

(3) Physical Stress

(4) Marital Stress

(5) Ministrial Stress (job stress)

(6) Spiritual Stress (sin, no peace for the wicked)

(7) Social Stress (peer pressure)

(8) Physiological Stress (high blood pressure)

STRESS

Stress ranges from a low-zone to a high-zone (1- 10).

There are two categories of stress: distress (negative stress) and eustress (positive stress).

Eustress is what energizes us and motivates us to make a change. e.g. Abraham & Lot (Genesis 13:5-7)

Distress involves negative feelings and is often a difficult experience

SYMPTOMS OF STRESS

Anxiety/Worry

Fear

Anger

Sadness

Irritation (overreaction)

Frustration

Depression

Sleeplessness

Restlessness

High Blood Pressure

CAUSES OF STRESS

Anything that puts pressure on a person that may feel overwhelming can cause stress.

Major stressors include:

Changing jobs

Job loss

Moving

Traffic

Money (lack or too much)

Bad News

Traumatic events like natural disasters and car accidents

CAUSES OF STRESS - contd.

Too much work

Long hours at work

Financial obligations

Problems at work/home

Unrealistic expectations

Going through a divorce

Death of a loved one

Hosting visitors

Going to school while working

CAUSES OF STRESS - contd.

Pregnancy

Parenting/ raising kids

Not having enough rest (Sabbath)

Urgent deadlines

Lack of cooperation (at work/home)

Lack of some necessity

Preparing for an important occasion such as wedding

Taking an exam

STRESS MANAGEMENT

Stress management offers a range of strategies to help you better deal with stress and difficulty (adversity) in your life.

The strategies are aimed at controlling a person's level of stress.

SM helps you break the hold stress has on your life, so you can be happier, healthier, and more productive.

Managing that stress becomes vital in order to keep up with job performance as well as relationship with co-workers and employers.

Jesus went through stressful moments – John 6:15

LIVING ON A BALANCED SCALE

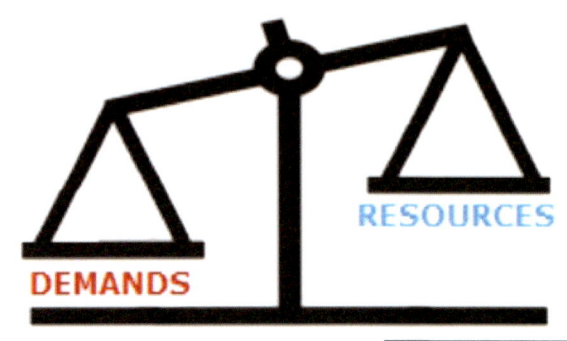

COGS OF STRESS

- Distorted Thinking "Too many demands" "I can't cope"
- Neglect self
- Do too much
- STRESS
- Life Stress
- No time for me
- Impossible expectations

STRESS MANAGEMENT TECHNIQUES

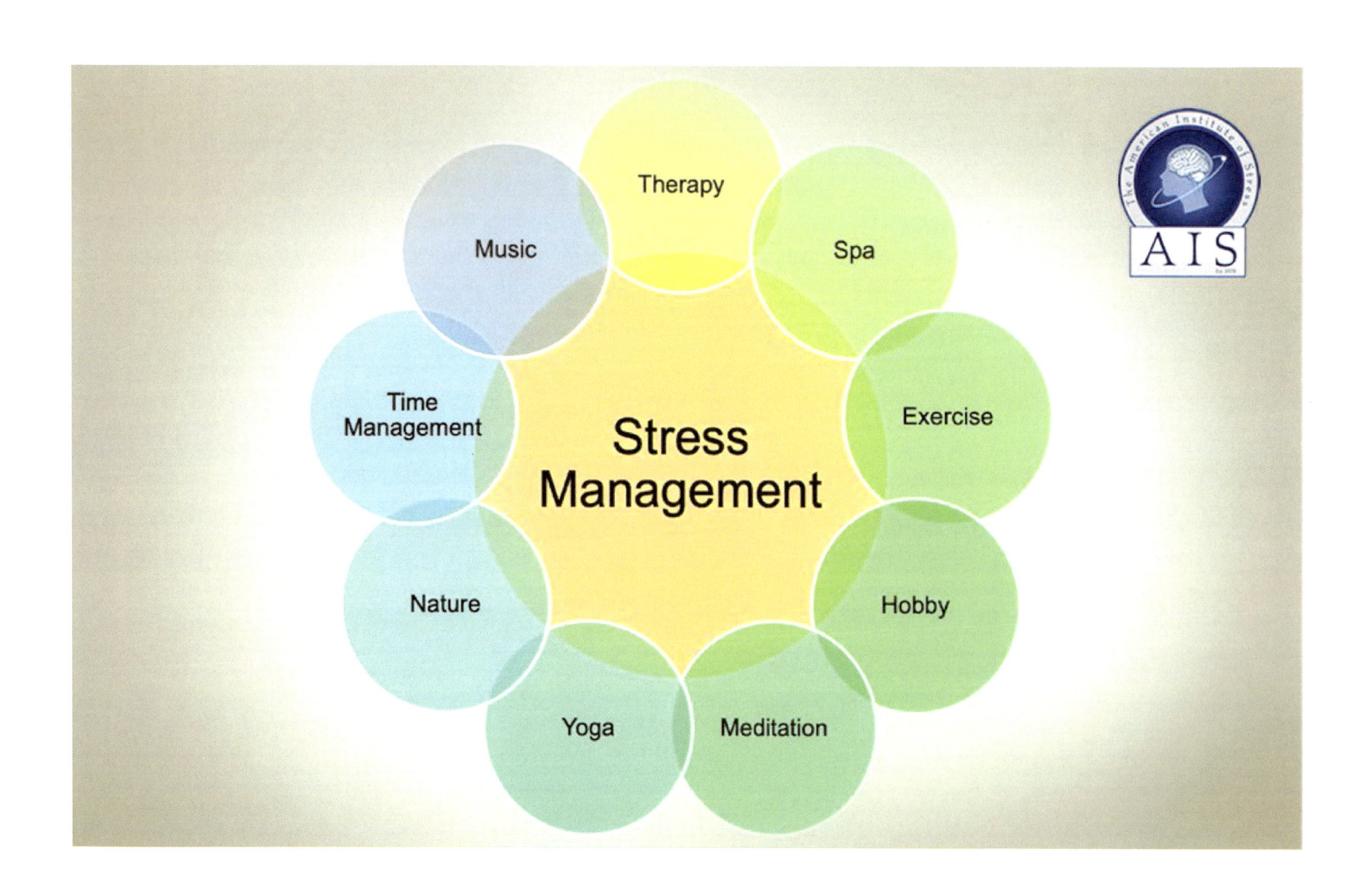

STRESS MANAGEMENT TIPS

1. Stress awareness

2. Identify and reduce sources of stress

3. Avoid unnecessary stress (or prevent stress)

4. Know your limitations and set boundaries

5. Alter the situation

6. Accept the things you can't change

7. Doing things differently: Reduce demands or Increase resources

8. Make time for fun and relaxation

SM TIPS - contd.

9. Getting enough sleep can help reduce stress

10. Manage your time more effectively (to be discussed later)

11. Choose a healthy lifestyle

12. Practice relaxation techniques such as deep breathing, yoga, meditation, exercise, and prayer

13. Check your blood pressure

14. Avoid sin

15. Commit your ways to the Lord

16. Have faith in God

SM TIPS - contd.

STRESS MANAGEMENT CONTROL

Meditation (on God's Word, Josh. 1:8) brings short-term stress relief as well as lasting stress management benefits

Exercise is a fantastic stress reliever that can work in minutes. People who exercise tend to feel less anxious and less stressed.

People who get involved in religious activities (dancing and praising God) experience less stress.

A healthy diet can lessen the effects of stress and lower your blood pressure.

Eating lots of added sugar and fat can have the opposite effect.

Drink less caffeine and more water.

SM CONTROL - contd.

A daily multivitamin may help address nutritional deficits and ensure you get the necessary vitamins and minerals to feel your best.

Distract yourself with music or podcasts.

Belly breathing helps lower stress and sends a message to the brain to relax.

Connect with loved ones and do not allow stress to get in the way of being social.

For chronic stress, see your doctor or a mental health professional.

Do not over-commit yourself.

Learn to say no.

Jesus hid himself sometimes — John 6:15

TIME MANAGEMENT

Time is the most precious thing in this world, even more than money.

There is time for everything. Don't waste your time.

Every individual, whether a student, professional, manager, entrepreneur or home-maker, has limited time available to do things. We all have 24 hours a day and 168 hours in every week.

Time is the great equalizer—everybody gets the same twenty-four hours each day. A day consists of 86,400 seconds

Time management (TM) is life management.

TIME MANAGEMENT - contd.

TM is the coordination of activities to maximize the effectiveness of an individual's efforts. Its aim is to enable people to get more work done in less time.

It is the process of dividing your time between different activities

Like Peter Drucker rightly said, "Until we can manage time, we can manage nothing."

A major benefit to using your time more efficiently is that it can help with stress and overall mental health.

If you manage your time properly, then it can reduce your stress level.

TIME MANAGEMENT SKILLS

Using Free Time Smartly:
Time to relax, but you need to be productive with your free time, too
01

Prioritizing:
Always more to do than time, so we have to prioritize
02

Delegating & Outsourcing:
Allow yourself to delegate the work that's not a top priority
03

04

Goal Setting:
You can't reach a destination if you don't know where you are going

Self-Discipline:
Learning & practicing self-discipline is a life-long process
07

Learn to Say No:
Set boundaries and respect your time and plans
06

Planning & Scheduling:
Saves time & boosts productivity
05

Source: "Time management skills," https://www.sketchbubble.com/en/presentation-time-management-skills.html

ADVANTAGES OF TIME MANAGEMENT

Time management helps in increasing efficiency and motivation of people.

It helps us to work smarter than harder.

Time management helps in cost reduction as prioritized tasks are given preference.

Feel like you have more time in your day.

Time management reduces stress and improved work life balance.

Better time management means a better work-life balance.

You can achieve more when you dedicate time to the right things.

BENEFITS OF STRESS MANAGEMENT

Managing stress can help you:

Sleep better

Reduced blood pressure/tension

Improved mental health

Control your weight

Have less muscle tension

Be in a better mood

Get along better with family and friends

Less sick days

BIBLE VERSES ON SM

Matthew 6:34: "Therefore do not worry about tomorrow, for tomorrow will worry about itself. Each day has enough trouble of its own."

Philippians 4:6: "Do not be anxious about anything, but in everything, by prayer and petition, with thanksgiving, present your requests to God."

Luke 12:25: "Who of you by worrying can add a single hour to your life?"

Joshua 1:9: "Have I not commanded you? Be strong and courageous. Do not be frightened, and do not be dismayed, for the Lord your God is with you wherever you go."

Psalm 94:19: "When the cares of my heart are many, your consolations cheer my soul."

Psalm 55:22: "Cast your burden on the Lord, and he will sustain you; he will never permit the righteous to be moved."

CONCLUSION

Stress is feeling overwhelmed in response to factors outside of yourself.

Experiencing stress can disrupt your attention, cause poor mental health, and increase your risk of disease.

As Hans Selye said, "It's not stress that kills us, it is our reaction to it."

Finding the best stress relief strategies may take some experimenting.

What works to relieve stress for one person may not work for someone else.

QUESTIONS ?

INDEX

Access to God, 120,121
Advocacy, 124,125
Angels, 105

Being radical, 6

Character, 158
Characteristics of a leader, 158
Characteristics of love, 38
Christ-centered home, 28
Classification of sermons, 112
Commitment, 40
Communication, 33
Communication killers, 34
Compassion, 159
Competency, 159
Courage, 160

David, 181
Disciples, 8
Discipline, 173,174
Divine order, 29
Dreams, 101

Effective communication, 161
Effective leadership, 152,162-182
Effective time management, 178,179
Enemies of commitment, 41
Energy level, 204

Faith, 11,158
Faithfulness, 169,170
Father, 113
Fear of the Lord, 165,166
Financial stewardship, 43,44
Focus, 175,176
Forgiveness, 67,116,117
    Characteristics of, 78
    Importance of, 73

Giving, 21
Glory of God, 142143
God, 7,10,13,14,76
God's will, 82
    Characteristics, 90-92
    Importance of, 85-87
    Meaning of, 83
    Perspectives on, 88,89
    Prerequisites for,93,94
Good shepherd, 138,139

INDEX - contd.

Heir of all things, 146,147
Holy Spirit, 97
How God guides, 95-107
Humility, 16

Importance, 203
Influence, 20
Integrity, 167,168
Jesus, 7,10,76
Judgment, 126,127

King of kings, 144,145
Kingdom, 6,10,152
Kingdom principles, 3,10-22,29,163
Knowledge, 160

Leaders, 184
Leadership, 153,154
Leadership styles, 155-157
Light of the world, 140,141
Love, 14
Love and appreciation, 38

Marriage, 26,66
Mature counsel, 99

Maturity, 42
Mediation, 122,123
Mission, 158

Names above all names, 135,136

One with all authority, 137

Parenting, 45,46
Patience, 180
Paul, 182,183
Prayer, 31,96
Procrastination, 200,201
Progress, 205
Prophecy, 107
Providential circumstances, 100

Radical living, 3,7
    Benefits of, 9,23
Reconciliation, 71
Righteousness, 13

Salvation, 114,115
Satan, 107
Scripture, 95

INDEX - contd.

Secrets, 27
Selfishness, 52,63
    Effects of, 57-59
    Manifestation of, 53-56
    Solution to, 60-62
Servant heart, 177
Setting priorities, 199
Signs, 102
Spiritual gifts, 106
Stress management, 211,221
    Benefits of, 234
    Bible verses on, 235
    Control of, 228,229
    Techniques of, 224
    Tips of, 225-227
Stress, 212
    Categories of, 215
    Causes of, 218-220
    Cogs of, 223
    Management of, 221
    Symptoms of, 217
    Types of, 214
Successful marriage, 27
Supernatural guidance, 101

Time, 190
Time management, 187-89,191,230,231
    Advantages of, 206,233
    Benefits of, 206
    Disadvantages of, 207
    In academia, 194,195
    In industry, 196
    Myths about, 193
    Skills of, 232
Time wasters, 202

Understanding, 35-37
Unforgiveness, 66,68-70
    Consequences of, 74,75
    Root causes of, 72
Unity, 18
Unselfishness, 171,172
Urgency, 203

Vigilance, 32
Visions, 103
Voice, 104

Wisdom, 98

Milton Keynes UK
Ingram Content Group UK Ltd.
UKRC030811301124
451267UK00008B/1